THE ART OF
NAUTICAL ILLUSTRATION

A PLEASANT BREEZE
William Lionel Wylie (1851–1931)
N.R. Omell

THE ART OF NAUTICAL ILLUSTRATION

A visual tribute to the achievements of
the classic marine illustrators

MICHAEL E. LEEK

KNICKERBOCKER PRESS

Published by Knickerbocker Press
276 Fifth Avenue, Suite 206
New York, NY 10001
USA

This edition printed 1998

ISBN 1-57715-032-5

This book is produced by
Quantum Books Ltd
6 Blundell Street
London N7 9BH

Printed in China by Leefung-Asco Printers Ltd

Designer: Bill Mason
Picture Researcher: Deirdre O'Day
Assistant Art Director: Chloë Alexander
Senior Editor: Sally MacEachern
Editor: Christine Shuttleworth
Index: Connie Tyler
Art Director: Moira Clinch
Publishing Director: Janet Slingsby

Typeset by Bookworm Typesetting, Manchester
Manufactured in Singapore by Bright Arts
(Singapore) Pte Ltd

Contents

Introduction

SINCE MAN HAS BEEN ABLE TO MASTER THE ART AND SCIENCE of navigation, the sea and the means to travel on it have contributed substantially to the growth of civilizations, in terms of exploration, expansion and trade. As with many other facets of life which have profoundly affected man over the centuries, both ships and the many moods of the sea itself have been depicted in paintings and illustrations – two-dimensional images which not only have obvious aesthetic appeal, but also add to our historical knowledge in recording specific events or man's technological development by way of naval architecture.

This book is an attempt to introduce the subject of marine painting and illustration to a wider and less specialized audience, in the hope of awakening in the reader an admiration for the artist's skill and knowledge in accurately reflecting as a static image an environment which is constantly moving and changing. There exists in these paintings an inherent beauty, be it of a ship, as a subject in its own right, or a combination of a ship with the eternal human struggle against the forces of the sea and weather. Of equal importance are the artist's sympathy, understanding and appreciation of his subject or theme. The paintings can and do tell their own story; the text is and must be secondary – a means of describing the context, the history of the art form and a biographical background about selected artists, not all of whom, for lack of space, have examples of their work reproduced here.

Not unnaturally, the development of marine painting and illustration, especially in terms of the subjects depicted, runs parallel with that of shipbuilding, naval architecture and, indeed, navigation. It is therefore unavoidable that a certain number of references to these other subjects has been made. However, it is felt that this will not in any way distract the reader from his or her appreciation of a sadly much-neglected field within the history of art as a whole.

The title of this book may cause confusion to some. Some of the almost theoretical studies on this aspect of the history of art normally refer to "marine art" or "painting". This has set a precedent, but without foundation, other

CLEWING UP THE MAINSAIL IN HEAVY WEATHER

Arthur John Trevor Briscoe (1873–1943)

National Maritime Museum, London

An excellent oil sketch, representative of this artist's lively and carefully observed style, showing an everyday incident during the last days of commercial sail.

RMS *MOREA* OFF GRAVESEND, IN 1913
Charles Dixon (1872–1934)
P & O, London

Dixon was an expert at producing large watercolours with a distinctive looser style, as in this example, which also combines very effectively the technologies of steam and sail in a busy river setting. Of particular note is the limited colour range – also typical of Dixon's work – and the apparent detail, which is suggested rather than actually included. Although the principal subject is the P & O liner, it is not the focal point of the painting, as there is some conflict between this and the sailing ship. Nevertheless the composition does, somewhat surprisingly, work very well.

than the fact that "illustration" is, by definition, a term used to explain something, by example or by imagery. In the context of this book, the word illustration is appropriate, for the reproductions represent the means by which the artists have tried to explain what they wished the viewer to see. In fact, the majority of the works reproduced here have been specifically chosen because they demonstrate the artists' skill not only as painters, but also because of what they are depicting. (It is partly because of this that abstract paintings have not been included, for they do not conform to the implications and definitions of the title of the book.) "Nautical" specifically refers to seamen and the art of navigation, while "marine" has been directly associated only with those who have specialized in painting the sea and ships since 1883, even though the word dates back to Old French. It can therefore be argued that, in a broad sense, the two words are interchangeable, so any confusion here should be limited.

It has been a primary aim to use works which have not been excessively reproduced before. As will become apparent, there are notable exceptions to this objective, for which no apology is made or offered, in the cases of works of such profound importance in the development of marine art that to omit them would be tantamount to sacrilege. They are also internationally recognized as being representative of the "state of the art" at the time they were first exhibited, and have remained outstanding examples. It was also decided to include only works by deceased artists, since the number of excellent contemporary living artists on both sides of the Atlantic would be sufficient for a separate book. Any selection is bound to contain an element of subjectivity or self-indulgence; however, it is to be hoped that those works reproduced here represent a reasonably broad cross-section, within the definition of the word illustration, even though the emphasis is on the past 200 years.

The concept of marine painting and illustration should not be seen purely in terms of ships at sea, as is so often the case in books on the subject. Rather, it embraces anything related to the sea, including paintings of those whose lives and employment, either directly or indirectly, are inextricably linked with the sea. If marine painting and illustration are seen to encompass the broader canvas suggested here, the scope for further study beyond the accepted routes and an enriched appreciation will be greatly enhanced. An attempt has been made to reflect this important broadening of the subject, which might prompt others to rethink their approach and produce new studies accordingly.

There are few, if any, extensive studies on the subject of marine painting which include such a large number of full-colour reproductions, which is very much to the credit of my publishers. Nevertheless, it has still not been possible to achieve a perfect balance, especially in a general survey such as this, covering the periods and time

◁ A SMELT NET FISHERMAN IN FALMOUTH HARBOUR
Charles Napier Hemy (1841–1917)
N.R. Omell Galleries, London
An outstanding example of the marine painter's art from one of the great practitioners. This beautifully observed and carefully balanced painting is representative of Hemy's fascination with coastal scenes and fishermen about their daily business near the harbour where he made his home.

A YACHT RUNNING IN A STIFF BREEZE
Montague Dawson (1895–1973)
Royal Exchange Art Gallery, London
This watercolour demonstrates Dawson's earlier and superior style, used before he developed the technique for which he is more widely known. There is nothing excessive or in conflict with nature; the whole painting is particularly pleasing, and it is a great shame he did not continue to produce such carefully composed images.

span which it does. Indeed the restraints imposed have not always been those of the book itself, but are the result of rigid and sometimes excessive transparency and reproduction fees laid down by many museums and collections around the world. This also accounts in part for the fact that the vast majority of the reproductions are by artists from Great Britain. Sadly, it is probable that, without the generosity of a small number of private galleries and far-sighted curators of public collections, it will become impossible to publish books like this, thereby depriving a wide audience of the experience of seeing and understanding such beautiful and inspiring works of art.

Any factual errors which may have crept into the text or captions will be mine, and for which I can only apologize; any statements or observations on the quality or otherwise of a particular artist's works are also mine, but these I defend in the belief that while my criticisms may be seen by some as being subjective, they are offered with sincerity and a personal conviction about what marine painting and illustration *should* be about – or at least what it should and does do for me. In addition, the criticisms and observations should be seen in the context of the scope of this book. Ultimately, art appreciation is very much about what appeals to the values and senses of the individual rather than any imposed doctrines formulated through generations of studies on the history of art.

The writing of this book and the selection of the paintings has been a stimulating experience which has left me in even greater awe of the incredible aptitude demonstrated by many of the artists. Having personally experienced sometimes insurmountable difficulties in rendering the sea and sky, regardless of medium, I can appreciate the efforts and single-mindedness in the pursuit of success of the artists whose works now follow. I hope this book inspires similar appreciation in my readers.

Michael E. Leek

Michael E. Leek
East Burton, Dorset
England

C H A P T E R O N E

Early Developments 2000 BC–AD 1600

As with many of man's early artistic developments it is in the lands whose shores lie on the Mediterranean Sea that we find some of the earliest recorded examples of the use of ships and boats as either a feature or backdrop in paintings. No doubt there exist earlier examples, but the ability or need to record either an event at sea or the movement of the sea itself had not been established as a clearly identifiable art form. In fact it was to be a long time in coming. Nevertheless, the Egyptians have left us with mural paintings depicting the boats they used on the Nile and in the eastern Mediterranean for either coastal exploration or trade. Of particular note is one from the tomb of Huy, Thebes, dating from *c.*1360 BC. As with all paintings left by the Egyptians, it shows their complete

lack of knowledge of the theory and application of perspective, and depicts the port side of a vessel with an almost draughtsmanlike accuracy. Even older are the crude images of sailing and oared craft which appear in murals, on vases and as carved reliefs in stone.

Following the Egyptians, the other great civilizations founded on the shores of the Mediterranean, those of the Phoenicians, Greeks and Romans, the latter two being known as the classical period, also provide us with early examples of maritime art, albeit in varying degrees. For example, the Greeks were not only fond of using images of their boats on vases and in reliefs, but also often depicted their mythological figures against a seascape. Seascapes also appear regularly as a feature in Greek narrative and anecdotal art. The Phoenicians, a great seafaring and gifted Semitic people, preceding the Greeks, have unfortunately left little evidence of their art forms, beyond a few stone reliefs and murals.

Of primary interest to the artists of this extensive era were the human form and human activities, which meant that the concept of landscape painting, almost for its own sake, developed to an extent not apparent with seascapes. This is particularly true of the Romans. However, in time they did extend their skills to the point where they were able to convey with reasonable conviction a sense of depth in their paintings, as well as capture the expanse of the sea. Besides the mosaics of Roman ships which have

THE VICE-REGAL BARGE FROM THE TOMB OF HUY, THEBES, *c.* 1360 BC
Copy by Mrs Nina de Garis Davies
British Museum, London
A watercolour and gouache copy from the original mural painting, showing the strict orthographic method of depicting ships during the time of the great Egyptian dynasties.

△ ROMAN WARSHIP MOSAIC
Sousse Museum, Tunisia
This second century AD mosaic shows a Roman warship with its oars, rigging and boarding plank.

▷ **THE SHIP OF ODYSSEUS PASSING THE SIRENS**
Greek red-figured vase, *c.*490–60BC, from Vulci, Etruria
British Museum, London

survived, there are mural paintings held in the Vatican Library, and dating from the 1st century BC, depicting scenes from the *Odyssey*, which show specific seascapes and the use of the sea as a backdrop. While these may be somewhat lacking in artistic skill by much later standards, there can be no doubt that they demonstrate understanding of the portrayal of the sea and the surrounding shoreline or cliff-faces.

There is no correlation – or at least insufficient evidence of correlation – between artistic developments from the Mediterranean countries and from lands in northern waters, such as the North Sea and the Baltic Sea. No doubt as a result of what were then considered vast distances, and the fact that the civilizations in the Mediterranean were much more advanced, each appears to have progressed independently of the other. The period known in Northern Europe as the Stone Age has given us stone carvings of skin-covered boats and vessels now commonly called longships. Unfortunately, little other evidence remains of whatever artistic skills might have existed during this period.

THE MIDDLE AGES

It is not until the Early and Later Middle Ages (1066–1485) that ships and the sea become more prominent in paintings and other forms of representation. The successful crossing of the English Channel and the subsequent invasion of England near Hastings in 1066 by William the Conqueror, Duke of Normandy, gave rise to the production of one of the most famous images of vessels at sea; the Bayeux Tapestry. This renowned example of Anglo-Saxon embroidery was produced in the latter half of the 11th century for the Bishop of Bayeux, who was a half-brother

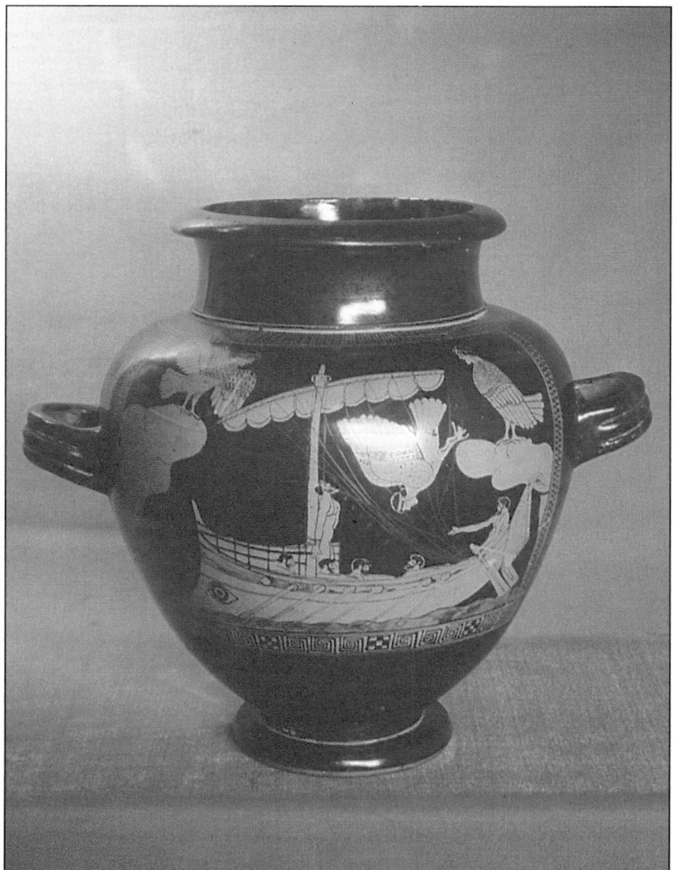

of William. Recent theories suggest that, unlike the majority of medieval art which was commissioned by and for the Church, this is in fact a rare example of the secular art of its period, there being little in the way of profound religious statements contained within it. It was probably embroidered at Canterbury and in its present, and unfinished state, measures 19 in deep by 230 ft long (48.2 cm by 70.15 m). It comprises 79 scenes and includes not only the invasion, but also the events leading up to it. As an embroidered illustration explaining a sequence of events, it is, for its time, unsurpassed; the eight colours, while used primarily for decorative purposes, show a subtle and carefully controlled application. The vessels are crudely but accurately depicted, conveying the comparative simplicity and small scale of vessels at this time, and, as with the Egyptian images, are shown in only two dimensions.

As is usual for this period, the Bible, from Noah's Ark to the many references to fishing in the New Testament, forms a major source of subject material, most often through illuminated manuscripts. Those which have survived show the illustrators as having only a very basic knowledge of ships and rigging; no doubt they were drawn by men living under strict religious orders in insular communities, whose main function was to convey in graphic terms the point of a particular story, rather than accuracy of detail. However, as design images combining the use of hand-drawn lettering with illustrations they are often extremely pleasing.

Apart from Biblical images, early expeditions were also featured in illuminated manuscripts. A particularly colourful example from the late 15th-century French manuscript, *Chronicles of Froissart*, shows the expedition of the Duc de Bourbon to Barbary. Again the vessels are shown as flat, two-dimensional images with simplified rigs, but at least an attempt has been made to give depth and scale to the illustration by the use of foreshortened vessels in the background; the resulting image conveys the impression of a crowded and almost congested departure.

Towards the end of the Later Middle Ages, during the Renaissance (1300–1500) and throughout the Tudor Age (1485–1603), Europeans embarked on some of their most notable voyages of discovery and exploration. This produced an increasing demand for visual records, and also inspired artists to extend their imaginative and artistic skills to place before a restricted audience their impressions of these great events. This period saw the gradual development of the use of simplified perspective to render ships and boats in paintings in a manner more in keeping with how the human eye perceives them.

An early example of the drawing of a ship with depth and solidity is that by Bicci di Lorenzo, *St Nicholas Rebuking the Tempest*. It is an oil painting on a wooden panel, taken from an altar-piece and completed in 1433; it is now in the Ashmolean Museum, Oxford. The vessel is shown as a starboard, three-quarter stern view and although the stern shape and decoration are clearly defined, the forecastle is completely out of drawing to the stern, giving the ship a twisted appearance. However, the image so presented is a vast improvement on the flat representations from earlier ages. An attempt has even been made to show some realism in the setting of the sail, which is in the process of being blown out by the strength of the wind. The ship herself is running *before* the wind, even though she appears to be running into the storm as well, rather than with it! This could, of course, be artistic licence, and when one considers the purpose for which it was painted, it is unlikely that there would be many observers with either a knowledge of the sea and ships, let alone a knowledge of perspective.

Religious influences on painters and illustrators were not restricted to stories generated by the Bible, but extended to later religious events and individuals. Many of the paintings produced during the periods under discussion and using these subjects or themes incorporate the sea or ships, often in a merely incidental manner.

Pieter Bruegel the Elder

The famous Flemish painter and engraver Pieter Bruegel the Elder used his skills to depict both seascapes and landscapes, and we are fortunate that so many have survived. He was born in north Brabant *c.*1525 and, after an apprenticeship under Pieter Coeck van Aelst in the port of Antwerp, travelled to Italy via France, possibly for inspiration from the great Renaissance painters, although some authorities suggest that he went primarily for the scenery. However, on his return to Antwerp, Bruegel became employed as an engraver and painter, fulfilling the requirements of the prosperous merchants whose headquarters were established in the equally prosperous city. It was here that he developed his precise yet fluent technique, with the paint often applied thinly, allowing the primer to permeate through, giving the effect of glazes or, as in watercolour painting, transparent washes.

Despite Bruegel's excellence in both seascapes and landscapes, he had obviously developed an early passion for ships and the sea, for they feature in several of his works which would seem to have little connection with water. Typical of this interest is his inclusion of a fleet at anchor beneath his skyscraper image of the Tower of Babel, in the Kunsthistorisches Museum, Vienna.

Another example is *The Fall of Icarus*, painted in about 1558. The actual subject of Icarus is almost incidental to the painting, for it shows him having already hit the water, with just his legs visible. Immediately behind him lies a convincing rendering of a typical large ship of the 16th century. The ship appears to be shown setting sail and heading for the open sea after clearing either a rocky shore or a harbour. Seen as a separate entity, the ship is well drawn and, except for the mast-tops, was clearly drawn by someone with a trained eye, who understood his subject. However, when it is seen, as indeed it should, in the context of the painting as a whole, there is little relationship between it and the surroundings. This criticism of what would today be considered almost primitive, is of course unfair, because in the appreciation of paintings and illustrations we should bear in mind the age or period when they were completed.

Although *The Fall of Icarus* is typical of Bruegel's outstanding work, the drawing errors in the ship are not, for in a series of marine prints by him, engraved by Frans Huys, we have been left some of the most accurate records of the appearance of 16th-century shipping. They show a clear understanding of the effect of wind on sea and sail, as well as of the changes in shape of a ship when seen from different angles.

Bruegel eventually settled in Brussels, where he produced some of his best and most universally known work. He died there in *c.*1569.

As I have said, the understanding and application of the theory of geometrical perspective was not very widespread until the 15th century; this is reflected in the sometimes peculiar distortions in many marine paintings, at least until the 17th and 18th centuries. And this is regardless of the fact that Euclid of Alexandria wrote his

ODIN'S EIGHT-LEGGED STEED *SLEIPNIR* AND A VIKING LONGSHIP
From a Swedish stela of the 8th century
Museum of National Antiquities, Stockholm

book *Optics*, which contains the earliest theorems on perspective ever published, in about 300 BC! While there can be no doubt that many professional artists at the time understood what they were looking at when painting a particular scene, it is evident in their work that they had little idea of how to apply what they saw onto two-dimensional drawing surfaces. Drawing and painting conventions of the time, dictated principally by the Church, although not necessarily written down in guides or textbooks, also influenced artists in how their work should be composed and completed. Italy and the Renaissance saw an increased use of one-point perspective, which was greatly influenced by the work of Euclid and evolved from him, but this was usually applied to paintings of interiors and rarely, if ever, used for seascapes, at least not to the same degree of accuracy.

MATTHEW BAKER'S DRAUGHTS

Besides the more obvious developments in marine painting, the 16th century also saw improvements in the method by which draughts (or plans) of ship were drawn. Matthew Baker, a shipbuilder and the first in England to be called Master Shipwright, was born in 1530. He was the son of James Baker, shipwright to Henry VIII, the founder of the Royal Navy. In *c.*1585 Matthew Baker wrote and illustrated his manuscript *Elements of Shipwrightery*, the earliest work on shipbuilding to have survived, currently housed in the Samuel Pepys Library at Magdalene College, Cambridge. It includes a number of orthographic elevations of ships and details of these.

One of the most famous of these draughts is that showing the sail plan of a typical, but unnamed, galleon from the starboard side. The complete drawing has been executed with some considerable technical drawing skill, with the hull rendered in watercolours as far as the waterline and the masts, spars and sails in pencil outline only. This suggests that the sail plan was a later addition. One aspect of the hull drawing which does not conform to a true orthographic drawing is the way in which the cannons have been shown. Strictly speaking, those along the ship's side should be shown as a number of concentric circles, representing cannons facing the observer, but they have been shown three-dimensionally, and all pointing towards the bows. Those protruding from the stern, while not true orthographic drawings themselves, do at least look right in comparison to those along the ship's side. This confusion between orthographic and three-dimensional representation also extends to the gun ports, but it is interesting to note that to the untrained eye these drawing errors either are never noticed, or do not become apparent until after a lengthy study of the draughts where they appear.

Another watercolour drawing from the same manuscript shows the hull of a galleon superimposed over a drawing of a fish; possibly to indicate what was then considered the ideal shape for the underwater part of a ship's hull – although the relationship between the two is tenuous, and made even more so in this particular draught. The ship is drawn giving an *impression* similar to a modern two-point perspective view, with the horizon line equal to or level with the waterline. Although not a true perspective illustration, it is nevertheless quite convincing.

Even though these draughts were prepared to illustrate a detailed technical study and are therefore accurate "mechanical" representations, they do have a quality which is comparable to the more traditionally accepted concepts of marine illustration. The colours have been carefully selected and show a pleasing balance between the natural colours of the timber used in the construction and the highly decorative and geometric designs incorporated in the upper works, which are predominantly in primary colours. The draughtsman has also attempted to indicate the hull form on some draughts by the use of gradated tones in the region of the bows and stern. While the work is not up to the standard of application of the artists and draughtsmen of later centuries, the effect is convincing and clearly conveys the narrowing of the hull form in these areas. That they are watercolours and have survived so well is partly due to the fact that they have been produced on handmade, acid-free paper.

THE ARMADA

The attempt of King Philip II of Spain to invade England with the Spanish Armada in July 1588, and its subsequent defeat by the English, under the command of the Lord High Admiral, Charles Howard of Effingham, provided inspiration to a few artists at the time, and not just English artists. The event can effectively be said to have laid the foundation for what was eventually to become a very British tradition among marine painters in recording sea battles, either between great fleets or between individual vessels from opposing nations.

The images produced as a result of this great historic event are varied, from engravings to oil paintings. One of the most famous, reproduced many times, is that showing the Armada being attacked by the English, executed by an unknown artist. It is housed in the National Maritime Museum, Greenwich, and is a lively and colourful image, giving, at first glance, the impression of a fleet celebrating a royal visit or some such other cheerful occasion, rather than two fleets engaged in battle. It has been suggested that this painting was a design for a tapestry, or more correctly an embroidery, although what evidence exists to support this is not clear. If this was in fact the case, there are a number of reasons why it was not proceeded with, not the least being the sheer complexity of the design, not only in terms of the number of vessels but also the delicate

JONAH AND THE WHALE
Manuscript painting from an English bestiary, late 12th century
Bodleian Library, Oxford

and intricate carvings and decorations shown on practically all the vessels.

Besides the foreshortening employed to create the impression of depth, this painting also demonstrates an early use of what appears to be the colour burnt sienna being applied to the sea. In fact the use of blue throughout the painting is limited, if it was ever used. Of course extensive fading may well have contributed to the lack of blue, in its early form a colour rather prone to fading if exposed to long periods of sunlight. Nevertheless, the gradated brown, from a stronger tone in the foreground to a paler, almost raw umber colour towards the horizon, complements the subdued range of colours used to render the vessels. This gives it an added quality which is often lost in many other paintings from this period, usually because of the use of too extensive a palette.

The development of marine painting and illustration during the period covered in this introductory chapter is as extensive as the period itself. The nature of the subject – the sea and ships – in relation to the historical events makes it very fragmented, without an underlying and identifiable thread of regular progression. When one studies the subject in greater depth there is almost a sense that one is looking at a third- or even a fourth-rate level of artistic accomplishment. With one or two notable exceptions, marine paintings pale into insignificance when compared with other subjects or forms of artistic expression. From the crude renderings of the Egyptians to the more realistic impressions of the Spanish Armada, marine painting and illustration nevertheless show little of the advancement made in comparable areas of painting, such as landscape and portraiture. It was in fact a small but powerful maritime nation which eventually raised the standards of marine painting to such a level that for many years they led the world, and by so doing established a separate and specialized school in the subject. And there is a certain irony in the fact that the Dutch should be that nation, for they were one of the last to allow themselves to be influenced by the masterpieces and techniques which had been developed in Italy during the Renaissance.

C H A P T E R   T W O

The Influence of the Dutch 1550–1700

THE DUTCH PAINTERS OF THE LATE 16TH AND, MORE IMPORTANTLY, of the 17th century were to have a profound influence on the future development of marine painting in all other European countries, but especially with the British. Eventually this influence was to extend across the Atlantic and affect the early exponents in North America (about whom more later). No study of the genre would be complete without reference to the outstanding aesthetic achievements of the Dutch.

NORTH AND SOUTH

The tradition of Dutch painting can effectively be divided into two, one growing up in Flanders, the southern, Flemish province of the Netherlands, and the other in the province in the North, which eventually gave its name to the country which grew out of the province itself – Holland. The two developed almost independently of each other, with Flemish painting arising in the 15th century from the traditions of illumination and eventually reaching its peak in what is known as the Golden Age of Flemish Art. The tradition of local or regional influences on Flemish painting continued until the 16th century, when many of the great artists travelled extensively to Italy and experienced the cultural and artistic impact of the Italian Renaissance movement. With the majority returning to Flanders greatly inspired by what they had seen and learnt, a change came about in the style of Flemish painting which led to the medieval traditions being replaced and almost integrated by the Mannerist style. This is a style which is crudely defined as a bridge between the Renaissance and Baroque art, but more accurately as one which claims that nature should be studied, but never blindly copied. The original Italian Mannerists – led by Giorgio Vasari – who formulated the concept of Mannerism, placed the emphasis on improving the artist's perception of nature according to the idea formulated in his mind. In other words, Mannerism meant a "mannered", exaggerated or affected style. In the Netherlands this trend was centred on the important Flemish port of Antwerp.

However, in the North, the Dutch painters of the 15th century had to travel south into France if they wished to improve their techniques and survive as artists, for there was little patronage in their own region. Even after an artistic tradition had established itself in Flanders, following the presence of the court of Burgundy in the southern Netherlands, the situation for artists in the North was a long time improving. Nevertheless, there were artists who were determined to remain in their own home region and many soon became recognized for their outstanding abilities, which led to suitable patronage. Towards the end of the century the number of artists establishing themselves in the North had steadily increased.

The 16th century also saw the influence of the Italian Renaissance extend to the Dutch, although at a much slower pace than with their Flemish neighbours. This was initially through the important and influential Dutch artist Jan van Scorel (1495–1562), who travelled to Italy in 1519 and did not return to Holland until five years later. Scorel did not travel directly to Italy, but went first to the southern German states, as well as Austria. From Venice he sailed to Jerusalem via Cyprus and other Greek islands, returning to Venice in 1520, from where he soon went to Rome. Scorel's travels and the reputation he acquired in his home country eventually encouraged others from the North to travel, notably Maerten van Heemskerck (1498–1574), who, with others, developed the Mannerist style to an advanced level which soon became dominant throughout the whole of the Netherlands. By the end of the 16th century the most important centre of painting in the North was Haarlem, where the Mannerist style reached its most distinguished height.

SPANISH DOMINANCE

The Dutch as a people were to achieve much during the period under discussion, and these achievements were soon to be reflected in the rise to eminence of both their landscape and their marine painters. The foundation can effectively be said to have been laid during the Spanish dominance of the Netherlands under the delegated authority of the Duchess of Parma. For the most part she

A 3RD RATE IN A STORM, POSSIBLY THE *HAMPTON COURT* OF 1678

Willem van de Velde the Younger (1633–1707)

Birmingham Museums and Art Gallery

This oil painting is a typical example of the Younger's work – the detail and sense of movement demonstrate his thorough understanding of his subject and the means by which to record it accurately. The artist has shown the ship sailing out of the picture area, which tends initially to attract the eye to the left of the painting before it takes in the overall composition. This creates a slight imbalance and explains why this painting has been severely cropped when reproduced on previous occasions. Identified as the *Hampton Court* on the basis of other drawings of the ship, the vessel also bears some similarity to the *Captain*, also of 1678.

A GALLEON RUNNING BEFORE THE WIND IN A FRESH BREEZE, CLOSE TO THE SHORE

Cornelius Verbeeck (*c.* 1590–1635)

Christie's, London

Less competent than that of the Van de Veldes, Verbeeck's work is representative of the early-17th-century Dutch marine paintings, and this relatively small oil is typical of his style and technique. Of particular note is the limited palette, which contributes greatly to the bringing together of all components of the composition.

was allowed to govern without interference, but in religious and some financial matters, including the imposition of "advisers" to ensure Spanish policy was adhered to, King Philip II of Spain was not so generous, and this was soon to cause friction.

It did not go unnoticed by Spain that Antwerp was already a centre of international trading and had become extremely wealthy as a result, making the city the banking centre of Flanders. In addition, Amsterdam in the North, whose prosperity was founded on the lucrative and successful herring-fishing industry, was also rising to prominence as an international trading port. The principal professions were those of sailors, fishermen, peasants and merchants. The geographical location of Amsterdam was of particular relevance in its success as a commercial centre, with its easy access to England, northern Germany and the Baltic States, besides France and the Atlantic coast of Spain.

The monies being generated by Antwerp and Amsterdam had an attraction for the Spanish, who were experiencing extreme financial difficulties through, among other reasons, an almost total ignorance of even the most elementary of economic laws. Of course, their attempts to supplement their own insufficient income by calling on the understandably unwilling Dutch did little to encourage peaceful co-existence. The strong trading links of the Dutch with England, a sympathetic Protestant country, did little to help either.

Changes were quickly made by Spain to the system of government in the Netherlands in 1564 as a result of the rebellions led by the Earl of Egmont and William, Prince of Orange. Nevertheless, religious persecution against the reformist beliefs of the Dutch continued with an even greater sense of urgency, which only served to enrage the populace even more. With William of Orange maintaining his control and leadership over continued attacks against the Spanish troops from the safety of his German residence, the Spaniards were forced to resort to imposing heavy taxes on the merchants to pay for their own troops. This had the effect of uniting the people of the Netherlands, regardless of class or religion, where all other attempts had failed.

An equally important factor in these developments was the sea. The Dutch were, by necessity, strongly linked to it, and much of its control was in Protestant and pirate hands. With the active encouragement and support of Queen Elizabeth I of England, these seamen, or "beggars of the sea" as they became known, unconsciously laid the foundation stone of a new and important independent European state. The stone was laid in their capture of the town of Brill in 1572. By 1576 the actions of the Spanish troops within both the northern and southern provinces of the Netherlands had strengthened the resolve of both Catholics and Protestants to join forces to rid their countries of the common enemy. However, it was not until

1578 that events decided that the northern provinces of Protestant Holland and the southern provinces of Catholic Flanders, soon to be known as Belgium, should be separate political states, the latter retaining its allegiance to the Spanish crown.

The relationship between the historical context and the development of painting in both regions is interesting in that the reputation of Flemish art entered into a decline, from which it has never recovered, while the Dutch entered their greatest period. For them it was not a period of anti-climax or exhaustion, but one of enthusiasm and positive direction. There can be no doubt that the national pride which grew out of their success in removing the Spanish influence, and their eventual independence, contributed largely to the positive and highly successful schools of landscape and marine painting which have given the 17th century almost exclusively to the Dutch in terms of the history of art.

William Gaunt, in his concise but thorough survey of marine painting, identifies three separate and broad phases in the development of Dutch marine painting in the 17th century. They accurately reflect the events which took place and which had an effect on the life of the Dutch nation. At the turn of the century artists were inspired to record the events at sea which led to the independence of the northern provinces. This first phase included the quieter, but hectic, expansion of Holland as an important trading, colonial and exploratory nation. This was followed by a period of comparative calm, where marine artists became conscious of the moods of nature and its effect on sky and sea – an early development of an almost romantic notion of the sea. Gaunt's third phase is identified as the period in Dutch history when they were yet again at war, but this time with England. These three phases are appropriate in recognizing trends in the Dutch approach to marine painting, and further establish the link between it and historical events.

VROOM, PORCELLIS AND DE VLIEGER

Hendrik Cornelisz Vroom is considered to be the father of Dutch realist marine painting – in fact it would be reasonable to call him also the father of all Western European marine painting. He was born in Haarlem in 1566, the son of an established landscape painter, and although there were others before him who had painted seascapes alongside landscapes, he was the first painter to make marine painting his specialism. Vroom travelled widely in Europe before settling permanently in his home town in 1590; from here his works brought him recognition, fame and fortune. His work consisted primarily of portraits of ships, fleets and naval battles; he had little interest in the "moods" of the sea.

Vroom was a competent draughtsman and this is evident in much of his work. He also appears to have had an understanding of the relationship between a ship and the sea and how both would appear to an observer. His ships "look right" and, compared to that of many of his contemporaries, the application of perspective shows more than a superficial awareness. Additionally, his paintings show a meticulous attention to detail, which is all finely painted. One of his paintings in the Rijksmuseum, Amsterdam, executed in 1607, is entitled *The Battle of Gibraltar*, and has as its focal point two ships engaging each other at close quarters. That to the right has been shown at the point of exploding and much debris – including crew members – are frozen in space, having been blown up from the ship. This painting effectively demonstrates not only movement, but also the other previously mentioned qualities which Vroom was so successful in applying to his works. The structure and shape of the vessels are carefully observed, as are their respective rigs.

The Battle of Gibraltar has been described in one study of Dutch painting as a "bird's-eye view". This usually means, in less flowery prose, an aerial perspective. However, Vroom's painting is definitely *not* an aerial perspective. He has merely shown the battle from a higher than usual viewpoint, for his eye level does not exceed the overall height of the highest mast.

Although he did specialize in marine painting, Vroom was not averse to including the shoreline in his paintings if it supported the composition or, more usually, was a constituent part of the intended image. An example exists in the National Maritime Museum, Greenwich, *Ships Trading in the East*, which he painted in 1614. It shows five European ships under reduced canvas entering a port in the Far East. To the left foreground is a jetty or quay which protrudes from the shoreline and in the left background lies a castle built on the low-lying cliffs, with islands lying immediately behind. The ships are shown having come around the furthest island, the first of which is at the point of entering the harbour, between the jetty and the castle. Because the expanse of the sea in the foreground dominates this painting and tends to look almost black in places, the overall painting takes on an almost sombre mood, even though the scene depicted is one of peaceful trade. There is quite a contrast between the rendering of the sea and the ships, for in the former the treatment is loose and broad, while the ships show Vroom's careful attention to detail.

Vroom was also a successful tapestry designer, and his greatest achievement in this field were the ten designs commissioned by and for Lord Howard of Effingham, showing the defeat of the Spanish Armada by the English fleet. After hanging for many years in the old House of Lords in London, they were unfortunately destroyed when that building caught fire in 1834. Hendrik Vroom died in 1640 after a successful international career, which included commissions from the English and Dutch courts

◁ DUTCH SHIPPING SCENE WITH A 3RD RATE
Abraham Storck (1644–1710)
Christie's, London
A beautifully drawn rendering of what must have been a typical sight in the approaches to Amsterdam during the artist's active life. This oil painting shows the artist's aptitude in carefully observing the design and construction of the vessels, as well as his understanding of the environment in which they operated.

THE *RESOLUTION* IN A GALE
Willem van de Velde the Younger (1633–1707)
National Maritime Museum, London
Another outstanding and famous painting by the Younger showing the Third Rate British warship under reduced canvas. The quality of such paintings provides us with both an image to be admired and appreciated, and one which provides historically accurate evidence of the appearance of important naval vessels of the period.

and the Dutch East India Company.

The influence of Pieter Bruegel the Elder is apparent to a greater or lesser degree in many Dutch marine artists of the early 17th century, not the least being Adam Willaerts (1577–1664). Willaerts was also initially influenced by Vroom, but soon developed his own style. He was particulary interested in filling the foreground of his canvases with shore scenes full of busy human activity. Nevertheless, his chosen subject matter, like Vroom's, emphasized the important naval and historical events to which he was a witness.

The gradual transition from the strictly realist approach of recording specific events to that where the atmosphere and mood of sea and weather become dominant can be said to have started in the work of Jan Porcellis. It was Porcellis who placed ships and boats in a broader setting so that they became integral, and in some cases secondary, to the scene, rather than dominating it, although the importance of technical accuracy was never lost on him. Porcellis was born in Ghent in 1584, but migrated to Holland where he settled to produce paintings and etchings of seascapes. He also spent some time at sea, and although this was not until he was 40, the experience obviously contributed to the approach he adopted in his painting. Whether the desire to go to sea was a reflection of Porcellis's restless nature is not known, but he was unable to remain in one place for long. He moved many times during his short life, before finally settling in Soetterwoude near Leiden, where he died in 1632.

In contrast to Vroom and indeed many of his contemporaries, Porcellis used a restricted palette, almost to the point of making his paintings appear monochromatic, but actually in keeping with the reality of subtle colour changes produced by the environment of the open sea. Another important facet of his work is the immediate and apparent sense of space. No longer are we looking at great sea battles or individual vessels in what often appears to be the restricted space of a lake or river, but the broad, open sea. A particularly good example of this early imaginative composition is shown in his painting *Fishing Boats*, housed in the Gemälde Galerie, Berlin. It is a very small oil painting on a panel, and interestingly the horizon line is brought down to approximately 20 per cent of the total depth of the picture; so, in terms of space, the sky with its racing clouds becomes the dominant feature. Not only does this example project the atmospheric reality of the Dutch coastline – and, except for the vessels, reflects the impression one receives today – but it conveys a genuine sense of a North Sea day with a typical short sea being whipped up by a slightly chilly fresh breeze.

Jan Porcellis set a new standard in Dutch marine painting, becoming almost the teacher to an entire generation of specialist painters. He was also considered by his peers to be the greatest marine painter of the day, and his work reflects the changing emphasis across the

THE FIRST BATTLE OF SCHOONEVALD, 28 MAY–7 JUNE 1673
Willem van de Velde the Elder (1611–93)
National Maritime Museum, London
The Elder was an outstanding draughtsman and developed the technique of grisaille work – pen and ink drawing – to a high level of perfection. His eye for detail was exemplary and he was easily able to distinguish between the necessary and the superfluous. This example, enhanced by the addition of grey washes, was produced in 1684 when the artist was 73. He based it on a sketch he made immediately after the battle, although he was himself an eye-witness to the event; this was the first battle he recorded from the English side, having arrived in England the year before.

DE RUYTER'S FLEET BEFORE THE WIND, WEDNESDAY AFTERNOON, 19 AUGUST 1665
Willem van de Velde the Elder (1611–93)
National Maritime Museum, London
To select one drawing from the many superb examples produced by the Van de Veldes is extremely difficult. This pleasing example conveys the atmosphere and grandeur of a fleet under sail.

whole of Dutch painting. In some respects it is a pity that many of our modern, contemporary marine artists fail to acknowledge or have forgotten the importance of 17th-century artists like Porcellis. Even a cursory study will show that, on the whole and with some notable exceptions, there has been a steady decline in the quality of marine painting in the 46 years since the end of the Second World War. A reappraisal on the part of individual artists is needed.

One of those influenced by Porcellis was the equally outstanding painter Simon Jacob de Vlieger (*c.*1600–1653). De Vlieger was born in Rotterdam, where he started his career, but eventually moved to Delft, where he became a member of the Guild of St Luke. After a number of years in Amsterdam he finally settled in Weesp. As with Porcellis, De Vlieger's later work concentrated on and developed the concept of space over vast expanses of open water, often as a flat calm. His earlier work reflected the emphasis on ship portraiture, but his limited palette with its subdued colours and carefully controlled tones is evident throughout. De Vlieger did not restrict himself to the painting of seascapes, but also painted river, forest, beach and night scenes, although he is recognized primarily as a marine painter because of the superior quality of his works in this genre.

The development and progression of Dutch marine painting during this period is important, for with such a comparatively small nation it was rare for artists to work in isolation from each other. Not unnaturally those whose talents were quickly recognized as surpassing the norm attracted the attention of younger artists, who were often directly trained by their seniors or made direct copies of their work. This created a very strong line of influence from one artist to another, a feature which runs throughout the 17th century. And of course, even though the century brought with it the usual crop of wars and intense political intrigue, it did not prevent the Dutch painters – or indeed any other painters – from moving around, especially to England, where their work came under the eyes of a wider audience, and with such movement their reputation and influence was sure to spread.

JAN VAN DE CAPELLE

We have seen how the influence of one artist led to the development of the work of another along similar lines,

with a gradual improvement or enhancement taking place as skills, perception and awareness increased. The self-taught Amsterdam painter Jan van de Capelle (*c.*1624–79) was no exception and although his profession was as a successful and wealthy dyer, he painted in his spare time. He became a student of De Vlieger, carefully copying his work until he himself had mastered the relevant techniques. Although Van de Capelle was self-taught, there is nothing amateurish about his work, and it shows not only a high degree of competence in the handling of oil paints, but also an underlying and advanced level of draughtsmanship. Like De Vlieger, Van de Capelle concentrated on scenes with vessels lying becalmed on flat, unruffled seas, usually at the mouths of rivers or in quiet, protected harbours.

Professor Wolfgang Stechow, the distinguished American art historian and one of the recognized experts on Dutch painting of this period, refers to Van de Capelle as "the greatest Dutch marine painter". Although he is not alone in this opinion, this is not a universally held view and is possibly a reflection of the fact that Stechow's examination of Dutch painting tended to concentrate on landscapes, and he was prone to make constant comparisons between the two genres, rather than examine marine painting in its own right. If he had done this, there is no doubt he would have come to a different conclusion. However, this is not to suggest that Van de Capelle's work is in any way inferior, for the inherent quality of his work makes him an important and significant individual in the development of Dutch marine painting.

Not only was Van de Capelle an accomplished marine painter; he was also one of the greatest art collectors of his time. His collection included not only seascapes, but also landscapes and portraits. The artists from whom he collected reads like a modern museum collection: Avercamp, Brouwer, De Vlieger, Hals, Porcellis, Rembrandt, Rubens, Hercules Seghers, Van Dyck and Van Goyen.

Van de Velde the Elder

As with many artists in Europe, Simon Jacob de Vlieger's influence extended not just to those painters who came into contact with his work, but also to those he directly helped to train. One of his pupils was Willem van de Velde the Younger, who with his father formed the most famous marine painting partnership which has ever existed.

The father, Willem van de Velde the Elder, was born in Leiden in late 1611, the son of a ship's master. Unfortunately little information survives about his early years or his training as an artist, but it is known he went to sea in 1622 on his father's transport vessel as part of the expedition to Grave, where he most probably met an artist by the name of Liefrinck. However, there is no evidence to suggest that Liefrinck influenced whatever drawing or artistic talent may have existed in the boy. Van de Velde the Elder married in 1631, the union producing two offspring, Willem the Younger, who was born in Leiden in 1633, and Adriaen, born in Amsterdam in 1636, soon after the family had moved there.

The first drawing attributed to Van de Velde the Elder is dated 1638, although he must have been producing work long before this, because by 1639 he was considered well enough known for his talents to be used as inserts below an official engraving of the action off Dunkirk in that year. He was also one of the earliest painters to accompany a fleet to sea and thereby witness naval actions at first hand. Among those from which he was to draw from life are the Battle of Scheveningen in 1653 and the Battle of Sound in 1658, when the Dutch fought against the Swedes. The Elder was also present at the Battle of Lowestoft in 1665, during the Second Dutch War, although it has been suggested that no commission was forthcoming because the Dutch were badly beaten. This would account for the fact that no drawing or painting exists for this battle by the Elder. The following year, in June 1666, he was present at the Four Days' Fight off the North Foreland, when the Dutch regained some of their lost prestige from the previous year by inflicting serious damage and heavy

casualties on the English fleet. On his return to the Netherlands, his drawings were approved by the Council of State and a painting commissioned.

Much of the Elder's work up until this time consisted of grisailles, which, loosely defined, means monochrome painting in grey or grey-based colours. More specifically, and with direct application to Willem the Elder's work, grisailles were pen-and-ink drawings on prepared gesso panels or canvases. Sometimes the pure pen-and-ink treatment was supplemented by the addition of grey washes. Many of the Elder's grisailles have survived, and remain a testament to his skill as a draughtsman and his ability to record meticulous detail without detracting from or interfering with the overall composition. Some are indeed beautiful, and it is a great pity that the publishers of many of the recognized works which include examples have allowed third-rate quality reproductions to be used. The only way to obtain a complete appreciation is to visit the various national collections in person.

Although not intended or designed for reproduction, these grisailles by the Elder are clearly 17th-century interpretations of what we would now call illustrations, for no other reason than in drawing them, he was explaining something; either a vessel or an event at sea. It is a clear link with the definition of the word illustration as outlined in the introduction.

In studying the drawings by Willem the Elder it is interesting to note the frequency with which the same viewpoint of a ship is used over a period of years. Indeed, this extends to complete compositions, with only minor areas or specific details being altered. Two examples which demonstrate this also demonstrate the varying degree of perfection in the Elder's drawing ability. The first example is *Two Views of a Dutch Flagship*, possibly the *Huis te Oosterwyk* (1653), from the vast collection at the National Maritime Museum, Greenwich. Completed in 1654, it is a beautifully executed drawing showing, to the left, and on the starboard bow a three-masted ship with her forecourse and fore and main topsails set, although the topsails are shown with their yards slightly lowered. To the right lies the same vessel, but shown from the port quarter and with the same sails set. The two views show the wind as coming from the same direction, as does the direction of the waves. To the left foreground is a section of foreshore with various figures, and in the background lie other vessels. Not only is this an outstanding work of art, but it also shows Willem the Elder's vast technical knowledge of ships, their construction and rigs. Composition-wise, the only slightly conflicting aspect is the foreshore scene, which interferes with the view of the vessel to the left of the drawing.

The second drawing, now in the Rijksmuseum, Amsterdam, was completed by the Elder in 1666. Simply called *The Four Days' Battle*, it was one of the studies he made following his eye-witness sketches. As with the drawing

described above, the principal composition comprises two vessels, the first of which is on the left on the starboard bow and the second on the right from the port quarter. The foreground and space between the ships holds a number of heavily manned ship's longboats, there being no foreshore. The background shows a number of other full-rigged vessels all from the stern or again from the port quarter, and progressively fading into the distance. Besides the positioning of the two vessels, other similarities are the almost identical number of sails which are set on both vessels. Again, neither has its topsail yards fully hoisted and there is more than a coincidental similarity between the shape and number of flags flying. The technical similarities between the ships means little, for in both drawings the vessels are of a comparable size and therefore there would not necessarily be much difference.

Though finely executed, this second drawing lacks the crispness and quality of the first. It also uses the wash treatment to a greater extent, and could in fact be a pure monochrome watercolour painting. The similarity definitely appears to be more than a coincidence, especially when one remembers that the Elder was present at the battle, so was therefore, one presumes, able to observe and record the relative positions of the participants with some degree of accuracy. However, when it is realized and appreciated that he executed over several hundred drawings and paintings, with some of the drawings being 3–5 ft (1–1.5m) across, it is maybe not surprising that an element of repetition becomes evident in his work.

While we are on the subject of these drawings, a small

◁ SHIPPING ON THE IJMEER, OUTSIDE AMSTERDAM
Abraham Storck (1644–1710)
Christie's, London
Storck was a popular and prolific painter, and it is suggested that in this example he used one of his many assistants to help complete the work. Whether or not this is true is, to a certain extent, immaterial, for the painting itself is worthy of detailed study. Some marine paintings of general scenes are convincing for reasons which are difficult to define; this is one such, for it is not hard to imagine the reality of what Storck has depicted, even if all the elements are somewhat compressed. As with the majority of his work, this scene provides evidence of his in-depth knowledge of ships.

THE DUTCH FLEET BEFORE THE BATTLE OF LOWESTOFT, MAY-JUNE 1665
Willem van de Velde the Elder (1611–93)
National Maritime Museum, London
It is not known for sure whether this is one of the drawings the Elder produced as an eye-witness. It shows the vessels of the Dutch fleet running before the wind in a moderate breeze about two days before the battle in which they suffered a severe loss, including that of their flagship, the *Eendracht*. The composition would make for a fine and more finished painting, but unfortunately extreme landscape formats were frowned upon at the time, as indeed they still are, even though the format lends itself so well to the subject.

but extremely important point requires clarification. It is an unfortunate fact that many theoretical experts of art history have no complete understanding of the techniques employed in either the painting or the preparatory drawing. This is particulary noticeable in some of the most respected studies which deal directly or otherwise with the work of the Van de Veldes. Reference is often made to their manner of showing vessels in "isometric perspective". This is a complete misnomer and a contradiction in terms, for "isometric" is but one way of depicting a subject and "perspective" is another – entirely separate. In isometric projection a three-dimensional image is created, but it is an image devoid of any relation to the way in which the eye perceives an object; it is a system of drawing which, by its very name, means that for all three axes there is only one measure or dimension. Perspective, on the other hand, is the word used to describe the impression perceived by the eye of an object or objects from a given viewpoint, and with each axis having its own set of foreshortened dimensions. It could be that what is in fact meant by isometric perspective is in fact one-point perspective – but the two *are* different. Indeed, this misunderstanding of drawing terms and applications extends to observations made about other marine artists, which can suggest an inherent failing on the part of the artist concerned when this is in fact not the case.

There is no doubt among all experts, be they practitioners or theorists, that the hull of a ship or boat lying on the water, regardless of the state of that water, is one of the most difficult of subjects to draw. This is especially the case when drawing from memory, without recourse to any reference source, and is based on the fact that for the most part ships are made up of numerous compound curves. It makes the identification of recognizable datum lines on which to base reference points for various parts of the hull very difficult, even more so when the knowledge of how the shape of a hull is arrived at is either extremely limited or non-existent. This must be borne in mind and carefully considered when reading art histories or studying the works of some of the great marine painters, regardless of the period – except to say that with the increased knowledge today of the theory of perspective it should be less of a problem to artists, but this is sadly not the case.

Besides the grisailles, many of Willem van de Velde the Elder's pencil and monochrome wash drawings have survived. They are worthy of extended study, if only to demonstrate his ability to record, with a high level of spontaneity and directness, ships and the moving sea. His carefully observed "rough" sketches of battle scenes and fleets manoeuvring are some of the most beautiful freehand drawings of marine subjects. The economy of line, detail and washes all combine to give a completely natural and free-flowing impression of movement.

The quality of Dutch marine, landscape and portrait painting had not gone unnoticed in England, and although the influence was very slowly having a positive effect, there was no indigenous school to provide for the increasing demand for paintings. So, when King Charles II made his declaration in June 1672 inviting Dutch artists, craftsmen and others to settle in England, even though the two countries were still at war with each other, it was not long after that Willem van de Velde decided to leave his native shores and try his luck with English patronage. He was also influenced in his decision to leave Holland by continuing domestic problems and the impact on his financial situation as a professional artist resulting from the long wars. He eventually settled with his elder son, Willem van de Velde the Younger, in Greenwich, London.

VAN DE VELDE THE YOUNGER

Willem van de Velde the Younger, who inherited his father's affinity for ships and the sea, was taught to draw by his father before going to De Vlieger, who then taught him how to paint. The combination of expertise from these two distinct artists, and his natural ability, gave the Younger a thorough grounding in the complexities of marine painting, which he was soon to use to good effect. He was a fast learner, as his early works clearly demonstrate, and although his drawing did not reach the standards of his father's grisailles, he achieved a more competent and fresher approach in his paintings (an obvious advantage when they worked closely together). Recognition of his competence and skill was not the result of the appreciation of later generations, but was achieved during the

THE FOUR DAYS BATTLE, 11–14 JUNE 1666
Abraham Storck (1644–1710)
National Maritime Museum, London
A dramatic, lively and inspiring record of a major naval battle between the Dutch and English fleets, shown on the left and right of the painting respectively. The composition is somewhat cramped, the result no doubt of the artist trying to incorporate as much information as possible. When it is compared with the sketches made by Van de Velde the Younger, the lack of space becomes even more apparent.

DUTCH SHIPPING OFF ENKHUIZEN
Jan Claesz Rietschoof (*c.* 1652–1719)
Christie's, London

An example of a marine painting by a lesser-known Dutch artist. There is sufficient information in this painting to suggest that the artist was familiar with his subject, even if the overall standard is not up to that of the Van de Veldes or Storck. The artist has effectively captured the moment of going about in the set of the sails on the vessel in the middle foreground. Nevertheless, although this is a reasonably competent painting, the composition lacks a focal point and the eye is forced to jump from one to another of the three vessels in the foreground. It must be pointed out that this example does not represent the best of this artist's work, for others survive which better demonstrate his abilities to draw carefully and render with conviction.

course of his own lifetime.

The Younger joined his father's studio in Amsterdam at the age of 19 and remained there until both left for England in late 1672 or early 1673. Before England, however, and during the latter part of his Dutch career, success did not prevent him from being influenced by others. One in particular was the equally important, German-born marine painter Ludolf Bakhuizen (1631–1708) who settled in Amsterdam and became closely associated with the Younger. The interchange of ideas and the teaching of techniques worked in many different directions, for Bakhuizen was himself inspired by the meticulous grisaille technique of the Elder, from whom he learnt much, and yet it was Bakhuizen who in turn influenced the Younger in his painting technique; some of the Younger's paintings from his late-Dutch period have been mistaken for Bakhuizen's, because the style and approach are almost indistinguishable.

In England the Van de Veldes received extensive patronage from both Charles II and James II, which included, from 1674, an annual salary of £100 to each. For the Elder it was to pay for his services to make drawings from observation of sea-fights, while for his son it was for converting the said drawings into oil paintings. Such royal patronage poses the rhetorical question: where might marine painting be today if a similar arrangement had been introduced since the Second World War? The contribution to the heritage of future generations alone would have more than justified the cost involved. However, this formal and important royal warrant as "official war artists" guaranteed a regular income to both father and son, avoiding the need to seek out patronage on a regular basis from other sources. As with many painters of this period, their abilities outweighed any sense of patriotism, for they also continued to paint for the Dutch market.

The studio in Greenwich which the Van de Veldes set up when they first arrived in England was located in what is now known as The Queen's House, appropriately part of the most beautiful of Britain's national museums, the National Maritime Museum. This was made available to them by way of additional payment through the offices of Charles II. In 1691 they moved to Westminster, where, two years later, at the age of 82, Van de Velde the Elder died. He had continued painting and drawing grisailles right up to the year of his death, and in the latter case did not simplify them to the point of omitting detail, but continued to maintain their highly finished character.

As I have mentioned, the Younger was the more competent when it came to painting. Not only was he able to master the intricacies of depicting ships and boats accurately, but he was equally able to place them in a setting which reflected his intense understanding of nature as applicable to the sea. The majority of his paintings are cohesive, integrated studies rather than just bland, technically accurate studies of ships or battles which just happen to be set in a seascape. Willem van de Velde the Younger was undoubtedly the greatest marine painter of the 17th century, and it has been suggested, with some justification, that no marine painter in the next 150 years was not influenced by his work in one way or another. The Younger died at Greenwich in April 1707.

No study of Dutch marine painting in general and the Van de Veldes in particular can even be attempted without recourse to three worthwhile and indeed beautifully produced studies. They are the two-volume work, *Van de Velde Drawings*, catalogued by Michael S. Robinson and published in 1973 and 1974; and his *magnum opus*, *The Paintings of the Willem van de Veldes*, also in two volumes and published in 1990. This latter book is an exemplary and scholarly work, but has a major weakness in that the works have been reproduced so ridiculously small, which does little justice to them. The final work worthy of particular note is the American author Frank Fox's study *Great Ships: the Battlefleet of King Charles II*, published in 1980; and here the reproductions have been printed in a more suitable and appropriate size, allowing a more realistic appraisal to be made of the Van de Veldes' skills.

Our understanding of the development of naval architecture and in particular the decoration and general appearance of named English and Dutch ships during the course of the 17th century owes much to the prolific output of the Van de Veldes. Much of the 18th century is, in comparison, a dark age, for our knowledge from this century is practically non-existent.

In the field of Dutch 17th-century marine drawing and painting, the Van de Veldes are often thought of as being the only dominant artists. While their contribution to the development of marine painting cannot be denied or ignored, it must not be forgotten that there were, in England and in Holland, many others who were making a notable contribution. Their work should be examined in parallel, and it is an unfortunate oversight by art historians that no detailed study has yet been made which concentrates and encompasses the whole of the Dutch marine painting school in the 17th century.

C H A P T E R   T H R E E

European Developments during the 17th and 18th Centuries 1650–1820

WHILE THE DUTCH WERE QUICKLY ESTABLISHING A CLEARLY identifiable school of marine painting during the course of the 17th century, it was to be some considerable time before their influence was to have an effect elsewhere. The standards in both drawing and painting were, at times, almost crude by comparison, especially during the latter part of the century.

In France the emphasis in painting was on the classical subjects demanded by the opulence and grandeur of the autocratic reign of Louis XIV (1661–1715). This opulence extended to the way in which the French decorated their ships, which were almost works of art in themselves. The evidence left in the works of the Van de Veldes demonstrates the degree of decoration carried by Dutch and English men-of-war, but nothing could compare with that of the French. It was soon appreciated that the effectiveness of some French ships was being seriously hampered by this excessive decoration. A French sculptor and painter who is recognized for his detailed designs for ships' carvings was Pierre Puget (1622–94). He was born near Marseilles and apprenticed to a shipbuilder, producing carved decorations, and at the age of 18 went to Italy, where he stayed for about three years. During his time in Florence he assisted in the execution of some ceiling paintings in the Pitti Palace. Returning to Marseilles, Puget continued with the designing and carving of ship decorations, as well as ship portraiture. However, some of his designs which have survived reflect continued over-ornamentation, which were rejected, so that he was forced to seek further employment as a sculptor, notably at the Palace of Versailles.

One of Puget's drawings is held in the Metropolitan Museum of Art, New York. It was drawn in *c.*1668 using pen, sepia ink and light washes. Central to the drawing is a full view of the stern of the ship, while immediately behind is a view of the complete hull from the port bow. The stern view is effectively an orthographic elevation, but that of the hull is a three-dimensional view and it is this view which shows Puget's less developed understanding of perspective when compared to that of the Van de Veldes. This is especially apparent in the region of the poop deck and stern lights. Nevertheless, the drawing is exquisitely detailed and shows that great care was taken when applying the neat pen-work over what must have been a preparatory pencil drawing. It also clearly demonstrates French thinking at the time with regard to decoration, for some of it looks as if it has been stolen from one of the great French palaces.

Another important French painter practising during the 17th century was Claude Gellée, also called Claude le Lorraine or Lorrain. Born in Champagne in 1600, he was taught to paint by the Italian landscape and marine painter Agostino Buonamico (1605–44). Although widely admired by many painters of the 18th and early 19th centuries, Claude's work again lacks the conviction and natural realism of the Dutch School. It is as if he painted scenes from an imaginary and idealistic past, with much evidence of his Italian experience coming through in the style he often adopted when depicting architecture. He was not a specialist marine painter, although his work shows much inspiration from the coastal areas and ships of the Mediterranean. When still in his twenties, Claude returned to settle permanently in Italy, where he died in 1682.

FOREIGN ARTISTS IN LONDON

Although there were many European artists who painted the sea, coastal views and scenes of rivers, few specialized in marine painting. The majority concentrated on landscapes, with a strong architectural content and in styles which reflected the influence of the Renaissance and continued developments in Italy. However, in London and at the time when the Van de Veldes were practising, there appears to have existed a group of marine painters, although they were not indigenous to England but, like landscape painting, an import from abroad. And, of

SHIPS IN A LIGHT BREEZE
Charles Brooking (1723–59)
National Maritime Museum, London
An outstandingly beautiful example of a great English marine painter's work. This oil painting is carefully drawn and observed, as well as being excellently composed. The colour balance is also carefully controlled. All this is indicative of why Brooking is considered one of the most important of English 18th-century marine artists. The subtle emphasis the artist has given to the Second Rate warship on the right of the painting, by placing it in the sunlight created by a gap in the clouds, gives rise to the suggestion that this is in fact a named and specific vessel, though no evidence exists to support this. It could also be that Brooking was merely using his skill in creating a masterpiece of marine painting.

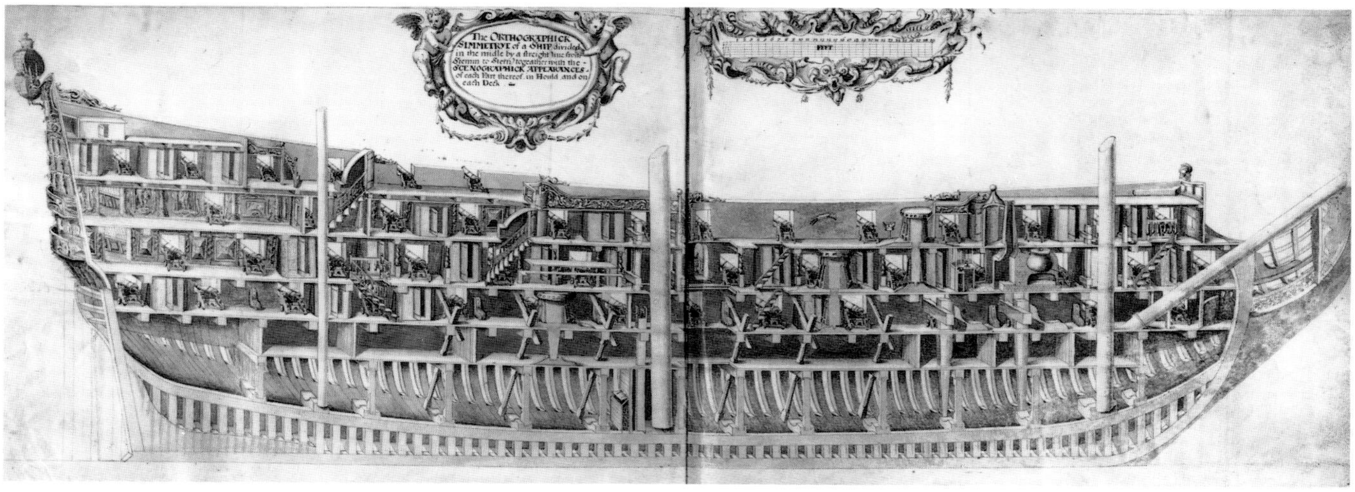

THE ORTHOGRAPHIC SYMMETRY OF A SHIP, ETC.
Engraved after Edmund Dummer
The Pepys Library, Magdalene College, Cambridge
An early example of the use of technical illustration to show a longitudinal section of a 100-gun First Rate warship and her internal arrangements. It is not a true orthographic elevation, for an element of depth has been introduced.

course, they were predominantly of Dutch origin, with the majority arriving during the 1670s. Significant among these artists were Jan Karel Donatus Van Beecq (1638–1722), Jacob Knyff (1638–81), Isaac Sailmaker (*c.*1633–1721), H. Vale (flourished. *c.* 1700–13), Cornelis van de Velde (*c.* 1675–1729) and Robert Woodcock (1692–1728). They represent but a small number of what may effectively be referred to as the first generation of British marine artists.

Jan van Beecq was born in Amsterdam and settled in London in the 1670s, and it is from his English period that the majority of his works survive. Although comparable in some respects to that of Van de Velde the Elder, his style is slightly idealistic in atmosphere, although the accuracy with which the ships are delineated remains. The Haarlem-born painter Jacob Knyff was yet another who took advantage of Charles II's invitation to go to England, and there is some evidence to suggest that he worked for a time with the Van de Veldes at Greenwich. His work often contains busy and lively scenes, depicting vessels invariably offshore or just outside a port. They are marked by the use of a subdued green tinged with grey in the hulls of the ships, and a distinctly simple, but effective rendering of the sea – in one or two examples almost pre-empting the style adopted by the famous Venetian painter Canaletto.

Isaac Sailmaker, originally from Scheveningen, near Haarlem, has until recently often been confused with Knyff. A close study of these two painters will, however, show a clear difference between them. Sailmaker's work is not as competently handled and has an almost primitive feel in comparison, especially in the way in which the sails are painted. His masts and spars also appear excessively thin, especially on those vessels shown with their sails furled. His work is inferior to that of the Van de Veldes and he was soon overtaken by them; however, he

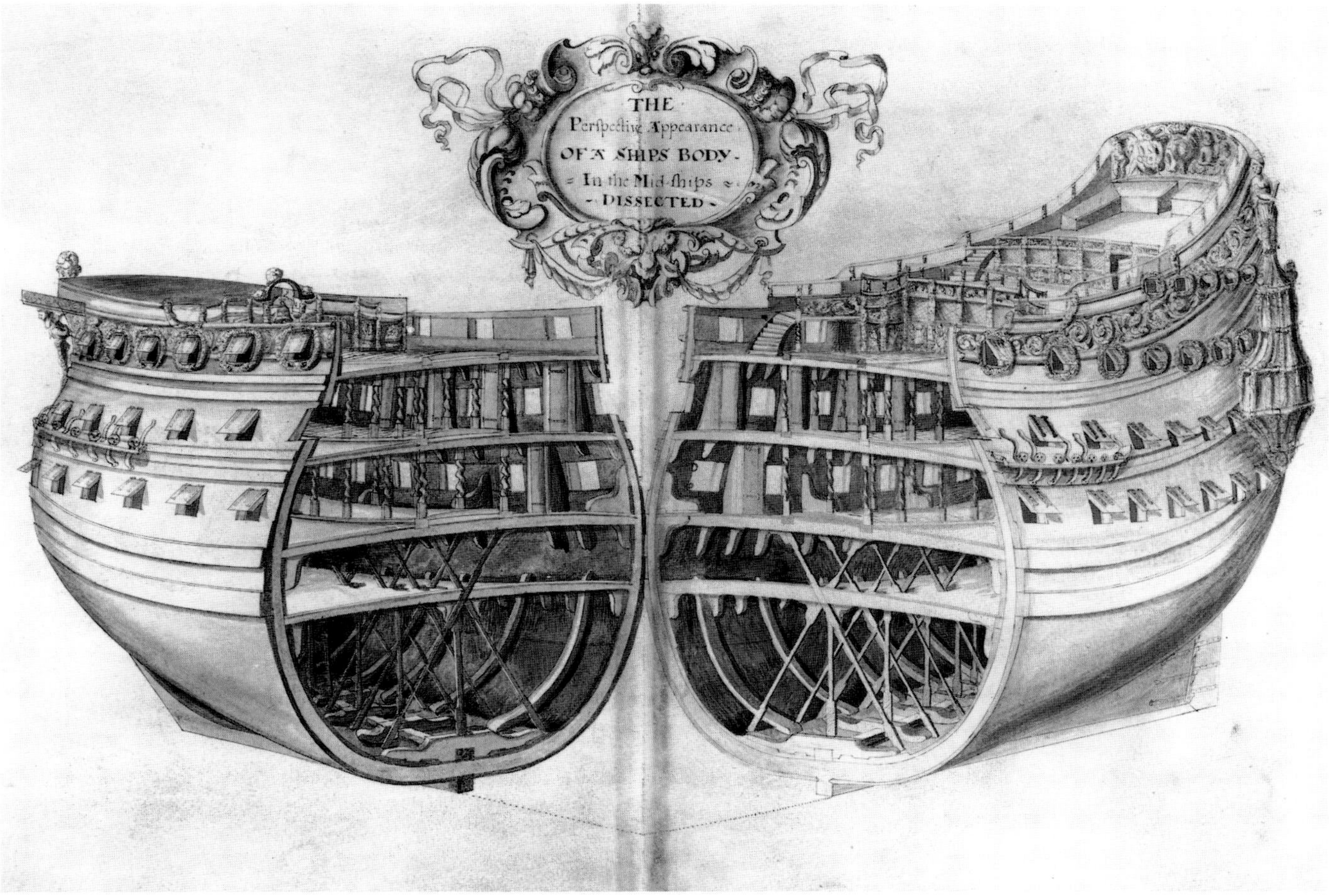

THE PERSPECTIVE APPEARANCE OF A SHIP'S BODY IN THE MIDSHIPS, DISSECTED
Engraved after Edmund Dummer
The Pepys Library, Magdalene College, Cambridge
In order to show both the midship section and central structure of this 90-gun warship as well as the ship's external appearance, the illustrator has chosen a somewhat unusual viewpoint.

outlived them and continued working until his death in London in 1721, at the age of 88.

Unfortunately we know very little of the life of Vale, whose paintings have the distinction of being identified as the earliest known of English – rather than British – marine painting.

Willem van de Velde the Younger's son Cornelis was born in London soon after his family had moved from Holland. He became an established and well-respected marine painter in his own lifetime, although the reputation of his grandfather and father has tended to place him as a second-rate artist, or at least as one not deserving the same degree of attention. Nevertheless, his work deserves to be recognized in its own right and not constantly in comparison with his seniors. A particular example showing Cornelis' lively and dramatic style, entitled *East Indiamen Driven on a Rocky Coast in a Storm*, painted about 1720, is held by the National Maritime Museum, Greenwich. The contrasting tonal values add greatly to the impression of violent seas and fast-moving clouds. And even though there are furious attempts by the crew of the Indiaman to the left foreground to prevent it, the impending shipwreck appears inevitable.

Originally a civil servant, working as a clerk in the Admiralty, and having an intense interest in ships and the sea, Robert Woodcock eventually changed careers to become a professional marine painter when he was 30. Unfortunately, he died in London at the age of 36, but not before he had developed his own particular style, resulting out of his copies of the Van de Veldes. A particularly pleasing composition is his *An English Third-Rate Getting under Way*, in the National Maritime Museum. Here we have a typical ship gently dipping her bows in a sea which can almost be said to be representative in style for marine painters of the period, but without fully set sails. Instead the ship is shown in the process of setting them, with her crew manning the shrouds, braces and halliards; in other words we are observing a typical everyday act of seamanship on behalf of a square-rigged sailing ship.

There can be no doubt that these artists all contributed to the development of English marine painting. But however hard one looks, it is difficult to come across many who matched the skill and aptitude of the Van de Veldes. There is an edge to their work, especially the paintings by the Younger, which constantly make them stand out and dominate.

PETER MONAMY

The first English-born marine painter of significance is considered to be Peter Monamy, who was born in 1681. Either English marine painters were lacking in ability, working in almost total isolation, or the influence of the Dutch was slow to reach them, for there is a not inconsiderable time difference between the achievements of the Van de Veldes and other Dutch-born painters and the work of Peter Monamy, whether working in Holland or in England.

Early sources record Monamy as having been born in Jersey – where possibly his father *was* born – but it has now been established that he was in fact born in London, near the Tower of London. He was apprenticed to a house decorator for seven years and developed a talent for the drawing and painting of marine subjects through natural ability and an intense interest in ships, naval history and the sea.

Not only was Monamy an accomplished painter, but he was also a skilled draughtsman. A beautifully spontaneous example of his pen-and-wash work exists in the National Maritime Museum: *A View of Deal from the Sea, South Foreland in the Distance*. This is a small drawing showing two frigates under reduced canvas in a fresh breeze, and has a great deal of movement for so simply rendered a drawing. It is vibrant and full of life. Although it is a pen-and-wash drawing, the use of the latter is carefully controlled with just enough to indicate depth and contrast. This drawing also demonstrates Monamy's knowledge of ships in a sea, for the vessel shown in profile from the port side is running steadily with the wind, while the ship shown heading towards the South Foreland has the wind almost on the beam, and she is shown heeling to port and dipping her bows into the beam sea. The detail shown is sufficient to convey the impression required, as well as enhancing the distance from the observer to the two ships, for at the distance indicated, detail would be less apparent. The inherent realism tends to suggest that it was drawn from life.

Whether this is so or not is not important. What is important is the natural drawing ability it clearly shows. Unfortunately, very often such sketches and preparatory drawings either do not exist, or they are not deemed as

NELSON'S FLAGSHIPS AT ANCHOR
Nicholas Pocock (1740–1821)
National Maritime Museum, London
This is undoubtedly Pocock's greatest masterpiece, painted in 1807 as part of a series covering Nelson's major battles. Although beautifully composed and executed, it is of course pure fiction in that it shows the principal commands of Nelson within the confines of a single anchorage, an event which would have been almost impossible to organize. The ships are, from left to right, the *Agamemnon*, the *Vanguard*, the *Elephant*, the *Captain* and finally Nelson's flagship at Trafalgar, the *Victory*. Aspects of this painting have been criticized by some, but they have misread the artist's concept and approach in realizing his aim, which has been perfectly achieved.

important as the finished painting. This is a false assumption to make, but the specialized studies of marine painting rarely, if ever, include such material. However, such drawings do require almost separate study, for they give a clearer indication of the artist's basic skill and understanding. This point can be better clarified when one remembers that so many artists developed their painting techniques by the direct copying of the work of their seniors or peers. This can lead to misleading assumptions when assessing the true abilities of an artist.

Another example of Monamy's work which demonstrates his excellent draughtsmanship is his oil painting *The English Fleet Coming to Anchor, about 1715*. Again this can be found in the National Maritime Museum. The first aspect which strikes one is the composition and the way in which a low eye-level has been used to add emphasis to the large first-rate lying to the left of centre, and viewed from the port quarter. The use of a low eye-level means that the waterlines of the various ships and the horizon would all appear, on a flat vertical plane, to be almost on the same line, but to create an accurate and realistic impression of depth and scale careful consideration needs to be given to the proportions of the ships and their masts. Monamy has succeeded beautifully in this painting. He has also combined his draughting skill with his understanding of light and shade and how the wind affects sails when in different stages of hoisting or lowering. Moreover, each of the ship's hulls actually appears to sit *in* the water, rather than on it or above it.

Peter Monamy died in London in 1749, after a successful career which has left us with not only an accurate record of ships of the period, but also a valuable and important collection from one of the founders of the English school of marine painting.

THE ENGLISH SCHOOL

The other great English artists who are deemed to have helped lay the foundations of a separate and clearly recognizable school of English marine painting are, chronologically by birth, Samuel Scott, John Cleveley the Elder, Dominic Serres the Elder, Charles Brooking, Nicholas Pocock, John Cleveley the Younger and John Thomas Serres. In general terms this did not become apparent until well into the 18th century, as the number of artists specializing in marine subjects increased with their own distinct if not original talents coming to the fore, and with the influence of the Dutch Masters diminishing proportionately. Not only does this period, and the artists mentioned, bring to the fore the British School, but it also leads directly into, and in some cases beyond, the Romantic Era, because the transition from one movement to another is never clearly defined, especially in this case. Those important artists who can more readily be identified as belonging to this latter classification will be discussed in Chapter Four, but it should be remembered at this stage how difficult it can be to categorize individual artists and slot them into specific groups.

Here I would like to note that many so-called developments, schools or centres of influence are the creations of art historians from much later generations, who have placed artists in particular slots for ease of description. The overlap from one chapter to another in this less specialized study demonstrates the difficulty in treating the whole development of marine painting and illustration (as defined in the Introduction) as a natural progression, rather than staying rigidly with the accepted divisions. It is very true that during their formative years as marine artists, many were taught by their seniors or influenced by their work, but whether they consciously placed themselves or their peers in the slots now allocated to them is debatable. It could almost be that the reality is nothing more than the fact that there were good, bad and indifferent artists who happened to have concentrated on the same subject-matter. This observation is very simplistic, but at least it allows the work of individual artists to be studied more accurately in the context of their own specific training, career and, importantly, their ability. And if one looks at present trends, these three categories fit very well – it is just a great shame that those considered good, regardless of subjectivity, are so few.

To return to the founding of an English School of marine painting: Peter Monamy shares the distinction of being one of the leaders with one other artist, Samuel Scott. Although he did arrive on the scene later (he was not born until *c.*1701, 20 years after Monamy), the two represent the link between the Dutch, under the Van de Veldes, and the first generation of indigenous English artists. Scott was very much a townsman, and this is reflected in much of his work. He was not a specialist marine painter, but had interests which extended to everyday life and the environment in which people in towns and cities lived; he was eventually to be greatly influenced in his architectural work by that great master, Canaletto. However, evidence suggests that he did venture outside to draw coastal and river scenes from life.

One of Scott's early marine commissions came from the East India Company, when he worked alongside George Lambert on six views of some of the ports and factories visited by the Company's vessels. Lambert was responsible for painting the architectural subjects, while Scott concentrated on the ships and water. This was obviously a successful collaboration, for Lambert and Scott worked together at a later date on a series of views of Plymouth and Mount Edgecumbe.

Scott's pure marine work shows a certain inconsistency of style and colour choice, although he appears to have retained his drawing skill, for the accuracy of his ships and their rigging does not appear to be the work of some uninformed amateur. He was fond of very dark, almost

THE FRIGATE *TRITON* AND OTHER VESSELS
Nicholas Pocock (1740–1821)
National Maritime Museum, London
Painted in 1797 for Vice-Admiral James Gambier, who designed the frigate and had her built at the navy's Deptford yard in 1796, this painting is possibly the second most famous of all Pocock's work. It has been suggested by some authorities that the two other vessels also represent the *Triton*, and while this would conform to the accepted practice when artists were commissioned to paint ship portraits, no evidence exists to confirm this suggestion. However, as a marine painting in general and as a ship portrait in particular it represents all that was excellent in the genre for this period, especially in England. Artistically the composition, colour balance and tonal values are almost without fault, while as a ship portrait it contains clear and undisputed evidence of having been rendered by an artist who clearly knew and understood his subject. The environment in which the frigate is set also confirms the artist's understanding of his chosen subject in the broadest sense.

burnt umber foregrounds which unfortunately tend to kill the subject. In other cases the natural relationship between sea and ship seems to be lacking, almost to the point that they are alien to each other. This is particularly apparent in his painting *The Action between the "Nottingham" and "Mars" in 1746*, in the National Maritime Museum. The same variation in conviction also exists in some of the individual ships shown in his paintings, such as two in the National Maritime Museum; the first of these, *A Danish Timber Bark Getting under Way*, shows a well-drawn merchant ship, but with one very serious fault – the scale, which is achieved by the inclusion of crew members. If this Danish bark was in fact the size shown in relation to the crew on her decks, she would surely have been one of the largest coastal sailing vessels ever built! The other painting, *The First-Rate "Royal William" wearing the Flag of the Commander-in-Chief, Shortening Sail and Saluting*, is more accurate in scale, but, with the exception of her stern galleries, the ship is static and without substance.

When one takes a fresh look at Scott's river or coastal views, or indeed any image which includes architecture, these are generally far more convincing and reflect a change of both style and direction. Of course, by comparison with his pure marine paintings, the ships are secondary – but still necessary – to the theme, and as such work better. An interesting and plausible reason for this difference may lie in the fact that Scott was not so attracted to the sea that he wanted to experience it at first hand. Except for one crossing over to Holland, he never went very near the sea, and his knowledge of seamanship must therefore have been extremely limited. This may also account for the fact that he rarely painted ships in rough seas or undertaking specific manoeuvres.

Developing gout in later life, Scott retired to Bath, where he died in 1772, at the age of 71 or 72.

The Cleveleys, Brooking and the Serres

Another important marine painter who successfully combined ships with architecture was John Cleveley the Elder. He was born in Southwark, London, in *c.*1712, and after an apprenticeship to a carpenter and joiner, settled in the Royal Dockyard at Deptford, where he was to remain until his death in 1777. John Cleveley became known for his distinctive paintings of ships being built and launched, and he was able to render both ship and dockyard with an equal amount of skill and accuracy. Obviously, living and working within a Royal Dockyard gave him wonderful opportunities to make preparatory drawings from life. These dockyard scenes are very strictly explanatory in nature and therefore constitute an important record for historians. However, they can become monotonous and are best studied in isolation from each other. Cleveley did not restrict himself to

AN EAST INDIAMAN
Thomas Whitcombe (*c.* 1752–1824)
Christie's, London

Whitcombe was one of the outstanding marine artists of his day and also made an important contribution to the recording of the naval aspects of the French Revolutionary Wars. His work compares very favourably with that of Pocock; though it may at times lack the quality apparent in that of his peer, it contains much which can be admired. In this example, the way in which the artist has depicted the ship reflects very much the reality of a given situation at sea and under sail, in that the ship is shown hove-to while it awaits the arrival of the long boat, which lies just off its stern. The fact that the artist has chosen to show the sails set in this way supports the theory that he was well acquainted with his subject.

NAPOLEON ABOARD THE *BELLEROPHON* AT PLYMOUTH, AUGUST 1815

John James Chalon (1778–1854)

National Maritime Museum, London

Although the title of this painting is self-explanatory, the subject is some distance off, but the atmosphere of the event is excellently interpreted and Napoleon himself is visible at the top of the gangway. The breadth of space and depth has been well captured, although the small cutter in the right foreground is too dominating and spoils the composition. This artist was primarily concerned with landscapes, even though this painting clearly shows his ability to handle marine subjects, albeit a harbour scene.

dockyard scenes, but branched out and made a number of studies of ships on the open seas. These again reflect his deep understanding of ship design, coupled with his accurate drawing skills.

An outstanding and highly gifted artist from this second generation of British marine artists was Charles Brooking, about whom we know little beyond the masterpieces he left. He was born in Deptford in 1723 and died, possibly from tuberculosis, at the early age of 36, in 1759. He appears to have been self-taught, and in his early years referred to the works of the Van de Veldes and De Vlieger, sometimes making copies from them, but invariably applying his own style and palette. While the influence of the Van de Veldes cannot be denied, sources suggest that his work has a greater affinity to that of De Vlieger. Brooking's work was not restricted to the traditional concept of marine painting, for at the age of 29 he was commissioned to illustrate a book on marine biology. This is evidence of the reputation he had built up, although it failed to provide sufficiently for him and his family, thanks to the way in which he was treated by an art dealer in central London. It is suggested that this dealer removed Brooking's name from his canvases to prevent his customers from discovering the artist's identity. Brooking's struggle for recognition and patrons was unsuccessful until the last few years of his life.

Subject-wise, Brooking was diverse, but unlike the majority of his contemporaries he did not produce set-piece naval battles. His marine paintings were more everyday impressions of ships going about their business in a variety of sea and weather conditions, including whalers in the Arctic ice. Whether his ships are on an even keel or heeling to the wind, the change in angle and the resultant change in perspective are all carefully recorded and beautifully drawn. It is difficult, and almost insulting, to try to find drawing errors in his work, for he was clearly able to visualize a vessel from any viewpoint and place it in the water with a confidence born from an extensive knowledge of the subject. With this skill so apparent in his finished paintings, it would have been an education to be able to study his preparatory pencil drawings, if they had survived.

It is interesting to speculate on why England should have had such an attraction for foreign artists, and why so many were to make an important contribution towards the English School. That the Dutch came over in comparatively large numbers, and over a number of years, is no surprise, but to find a Frenchman among all the great names associated with English marine painting is almost incongruous, especially when one considers the regularity with which the two nations opposed each other. Dominic Serres was born a Frenchman but chose to earn his living as an artist entirely in England. He was born in Gascony in 1722, the son of a wealthy landowner, and when it was decided that he should enter the priesthood, Serres ran away, going first to Spain and then to sea. His career at sea was not without success, for he achieved command of his own merchant vessel. He was eventually captured with his ship and found himself in England; it has been suggested that this was during the latter part of the War of the Austrian Succession, possibly in 1748, as a painting exists by him dated 1754. Serres's early movements in England are vague; some sources suggest he went first to Northamptonshire, but he finally settled in London.

Besides his notable contribution to the development of English marine painting, Dominic Serres has the distinction of being a founder member of the Royal Academy in London. This was in December 1768, although the concept had existed for some time. Indeed the St Martin's Lane Academy, which had been re-established by the painter William Hogarth in 1735 from the portrait painter Sir Godfrey Kneller's original private academy of 1711, had approached the Society of Dilettanti with a proposal for a Royal Academy. It was intended that such an academy would provide schools both of drawing and painting, as well as an annual summer exhibition. However, this proposal did not proceed, as a result of the imposition of conditions which would have resulted in control being vested in the Society of Dilettanti, rather than the artists from St Martin's Lane. These initial difficulties were not isolated, but compounded by unsuccessful discussions between other societies who were also interested in the concept of an academy, notably the Society of Arts (now the Royal Society of Arts) and the Incorporated Society of Artists of Great Britain. Dominic Serres had been elected to the latter society in 1765.

Discussions continued within the Incorporated Society of Artists, with the effect that the architect Sir William Chambers put the proposal to George III, who gave immediate royal approval. Thus, with royal patronage, the Royal Academy came into being; through it, the founding members hoped to raise the professional status of drawing, painting and sculpture, by means of exhibitions and formal training. Membership was limited to 40 Academicians, who were to be practising professional artists, and the first 36 were named in the Instrument of Foundation, of whom Serres was one, being chosen by the Incorporated Society.

For Dominic Serres this was indeed an honour, for not only was he of foreign birth, but he was also comparatively late in taking up painting as a profession. He obviously had a high level of motivation, for from 1768 until his death in London in 1793 he exhibited 108 paintings at the Royal Academy. He also exhibited 21 at the Free Society and eight at the Incorporated Society. In later life he became the RA's librarian.

Today it is considered almost an unwritten rule that marine paintings should not be submitted to the Royal Academy's Summer Show. This is a sad reflection on the hanging and selection committee when one remembers that among its founders was an active marine painter of some distinction. In fact there is now only one major outlet in England whereby contemporary marine painting can be studied; the Royal Society of Marine Artists' annual exhibition at the Mall Gallery.

In his work Serres tended, consciously or otherwise, to rely on a formula, especially in the manner used to depict ships. In many of his paintings the ships are shown under reduced canvas, which usually means the courses are furled, but the topsails are set and drawn with a degree of neatness which can only be artistic licence. This makes many of his ships appear stiff. It also tends to make the impact of one painting over another diminish, especially if many of his works are seen in close proximity to each other. Nevertheless, Serres did not restrict his compositions by having them dominated by the ships, but always tried to make sure they became part of the whole, which gave his paintings a sense of depth and openness.

Serres was very much indebted to Charles Brooking, and it has been suggested that he may well have been a pupil, or that Serres at least received substantial advice from Brooking. They no doubt knew each other, even though Brooking was unable to compete on equal terms socially because of his humble origins.

In 1747, John Cleveley the Elder and his wife had twins, both of whom were to receive recognition as marine painters in their own right. John Cleveley the Younger followed his father into the service of the Royal Dockyard at Deptford as a shipwright, but was always interested in drawing and painting. He received some tuition from both his father and the important topographical watercolour painter, Paul Sandby (*c.*1725–1809), who was drawing-master in nearby Woolwich. In 1772 John Cleveley the Younger was appointed the official artist to the naturalist Sir Joseph Banks for his voyage to Iceland. The watercolour illustrations he produced on this, and indeed the other scientific voyage under Captain Phipps (later to be Lord Mulgrave), on his polar expedition in 1773, show the Younger's careful attention to detail. One in particular from the second voyage, *Lord Mulgrave's Ships in the Ice in the Polar Regions* (1774), shows a good understanding of the technicalities of ships, but the painting is spoiled by a crude and stylistic rendering of the ice-floe. The figures too show a weak appreciation of the human form. Another, *"Racehorse" and "Carcass", 7 August 1773*, from the same expedition, shows yet another stylized interpretation of the ice. This particular drawing also gives the impression of having been drawn by an amateur in so far as the accuracy of the proportions of the masts and spars are concerned. This is surprising, for his later oils are well drawn, carefully composed and extremely competently painted, which is why he is considered an important member of the second generation of British marine painters. John Cleveley the Younger died in 1786.

His twin brother, Robert Cleveley, produced work of a more atmospheric nature, without the advanced draughting skills so apparent in his father's and brother's work, even though he received commissions from the royal household, including the appointment of Marine Painter to the Prince Regent. This shows the unavoidable subjectivity of any form of art appreciation or discussion. He died of an accident at Dover in 1809.

John Thomas Serres, the son of Dominic Serres, was born in London in 1759 and was taught painting by his father. He was very much involved in teaching throughout his life, even though he was successful as a marine painter; his achievements included the appointment of Marine Painter to George III and to HRH The Duke of Clarence on the death of his father in 1793. These appointments involved going to sea to record events as they happened, for which he was paid, in 1800, the substantial wage of £100 per month.

He lacked the more natural ability of his father, not only in his painting but also in the preparatory drawing, for John Serres' works often show peculiarities in the construction of his ships. His painting *The Royal Yacht "Royal Sovereign"*, also recorded as *King George III aboard the "Royal Sovereign" off Weymouth in 1806*, in the National Maritime Museum, shows one such gross error. The royal yacht is shown from between the starboard quarter and the starboard beam. This is confirmed by the angle of the ship's stern which, although in strong shadow, is clearly visible. However, if you move forward the bows present an almost true side elevation. This would be visually impossible if the stern remained as visible as that shown. Furthermore, the yacht is shown heeling to port, or at least that is the impression given by the difference in height between the starboard rails and those on the port side, in the vicinity of the waist. But the stern shows the hull as sitting square on the water, with no heeling whatsoever. Overall, this creates an impression of a hull with a severe degree of twist.

If it were not for the fact that John Serres married one of his pupils, his success would have continued throughout his life. But unfortunately his wife had "ideas above her station", and Serres ended up in a debtors' prison, where he died in December 1825.

Throughout this period, and indeed that before, youngsters who demonstrated an early ability to draw and paint were encouraged to develop their skills. This was, of course, easier if the father was a practising painter, but if not, and subject to the family income, they would be apprenticed to an appropriate artist or craftsman. This often took place just as the child was entering his teens. The concentrated and intense tuition which was then considered the norm resulted in a level of practice unheard of today, except possibly by retired amateurs. It is therefore not surprising that some of these outstanding marine painters achieved impressive results so early on in life, whereas today it is rare that an artist achieves recognition for his work until late in life, or more often, not until he is dead.

An artist who brings together the developments of the first half of the 18th century with that of the maturity of the early 19th century is Nicholas Pocock. For this reason he is being discussed at the end of this chapter, for his contribution, due in part to a long and productive life, is as important as that of the Van de Veldes in the late 17th century.

Nicholas Pocock

Nicholas Pocock was born in Bristol in May 1740, the son of a Bristol merchant and seaman. In 1757 Pocock himself was apprenticed as a seaman for seven years and by the age of 26 he had achieved his first command. This was the small three-masted merchant ship *Lloyd*, trading between Bristol and Charleston, North Carolina. Pocock's natural drawing and painting ability manifested itself while he was at sea, for he was fond of illustrating the ship's logbooks with delightful and accurate drawings of the ship. His logbooks therefore contain not only the cold, navigational facts of a voyage on a day-to-day basis, but a visual record is also given showing the ship's condition on a given day. Drawn at the same time as the log was written up, and by the master himself, these watercolour drawings have an increased value beyond their importance as paintings, but also as a major contribution to our historical knowledge of navigation and ship-handling.

In 1770 Pocock went to the Mediterranean in the *Betsey*; he completed the ship's log as before, but in even greater depth. On his return he resumed his command of the *Lloyd* and made a total of eight voyages to the West Indies, six in the *Lloyd* and two in the *Minerva*, returning to Bristol in 1776. Shortly afterwards he decided to retire from the sea to pursue a career as a professional marine artist. Until 1789 he worked from his home town of Bristol, concentrating on marine watercolours and topographical views in and around the city. After Bristol, Pocock moved with his family to Westminster, London, where he remained until 1817, when he returned to the region of his birth. He spent the last few years of his life in Bath and Maidenhead, dying in 1821 at the age of 80.

Not only was Pocock a skilful watercolour painter, but he was equally capable when using oils. His works are extremely varied in content, and while the majority are marines he also produced some excellent studies of the Avon region, Iceland, England, Wales and the Royal Dockyards at Woolwich and Plymouth, although his architectural works do not show the same confident handling as with those who concentrated more on this type of work. This is not in any way meant to undermine the ability or standing of Pocock, for it is far easier to draw and render a building with accuracy than it will ever

be to draw naturally and convincingly man's most beautiful creation, the square-rigged sailing ship.

Because he was present at the Battle of the Glorious First of June in 1794 and produced many fine and accurate studies in oils of this and other battles, Pocock's work has often been reproduced in books covering the naval history of the period. For a contemporary of Viscount Horatio Nelson, this is not surprising, but his drawings and watercolours should not be ignored. As with Willem van de Velde the Elder and Peter Monamy, Pocock's sketches are simply superb. Whether they are experimental tonal studies or quickly drawn sketches of naval engagements, observed from life, they exhibit an economy of line, detail and colour which gives one the impression of being a witness oneself.

An excellent and definitive study of this remarkable, self-taught artist now exists, *Nicholas Pocock 1740–1821*, by Dr David Cordingly of the National Maritime Museum. It contains many examples of Pocock's varied output, but unfortunately – and yet again – the quality of reproduction does little to bring out Pocock's invariably lively style. Furthermore, the number of full-colour reproductions in this book is limited, and in order to gain a full appreciation of the man considered by the present author the greatest marine artist of the late 18th century, it is necessary to visit the national collections holding examples of his work.

Pocock exhibited at the Royal Academy for the first time in 1782, submitting four paintings, and when one realizes that he was about 40 when he took up painting professionally, the total of 113 paintings he exhibited at the RA was no mean achievement. He received encouragement from Sir Joshua Reynolds, who was then the President of the RA, and this must undoubtedly have contributed to Pocock's decision to devote his life to painting. In addition he also exhibited regularly at the Society of Painters in Watercolour, with 183 works being recorded in a period spanning only 12 years, from 1805 to 1817!

His association with the Society of Painters in Watercolour, sometimes referred to as the Old Watercolour Society, was not just in the capacity of exhibitor, but as one of its founder members. The formation of the Society resulted from discussions between 10 watercolour painters; W. S. Gilpin, J. C. Nantes, Francis Nicholson, W. H. Pyne, Nicholas Pocock, Samuel Shelley, John Varley, Cornelius Varley and W. F. Wells. That eminent British landscape and marine artist Joseph Mallord William Turner was involved in the foundation through his association with Wells, but was prevented from closer participation by his existing membership of the Royal Academy, which at the time excluded membership of any other society. It was formally founded in November 1804, and one of its principal aims was to provide a forum whereby painters in this distinctly English medium could exhibit their work on an annual basis. The Society eventually received its royal warrant in 1881, since when it has become known as much by its initials, RWS, as by its full title, the Royal Watercolour Society.

The period covered by this chapter saw the gradual establishment of a clearly identifiable English School. However, it must always be remembered that to achieve an enhanced level of understanding and appreciation of marine painting, it is necessary to examine the work of the artists concerned first, and their school second. To describe an event or scene at sea involves much more than merely producing a painting which is pleasing to the eye. There are many other factors to be taken into consideration; including the artist's understanding of the movement of the sea, the ships he places on and in it, and his fundamental ability to draw accurately and convincingly from a variety of reference sources. In the latter case it has already been demonstrated how important it is for artists to have acquired a working knowledge of perspective, and how it can have a major effect both on proportions and on the way in which complicated shapes such as ships appear from different viewpoints.

◁ **A BRIG HOISTING SAIL, WITH OTHER SHIPPING**
Frans Arnold Breuhaus de Groot (1824–72)
Royal Exchange Art Gallery, London
Although strictly speaking the work of a 19th-century marine artist, this impressive and lively painting by the Dutchman Breuhaus de Groot is included here because it so effectively bridges the gap between the period of this chapter and Chapter Five. It is also a rare example of the continuity of the great Dutch marine painting traditions established during the 17th century, which unfortunately entered into a decline soon after. Of particular note is the most effective and realistic use of the sunlight on both the brig's hull and, importantly, on her sails, which is extremely well observed.

THE *VICTORY* CUTTING THROUGH THE FRENCH LINE AT THE BATTLE OF TRAFALGAR
Nicholas Pocock (1740–1821)
National Maritime Museum, London
This is one of many delightful, informative and natural watercolour paintings which Pocock produced throughout his life, this one being completed towards the end of his active career. Unfortunately it has not been possible to reproduce it in colour (apparently, it has suffered by being exposed to the sun for long periods, which has seriously affected the blue-based tints). Nevertheless, it is worthy of inclusion here if only to demonstrate the artist's natural drawing ability.

CHAPTER FOUR

The Romantic Era in Europe 1765–1848

THE YEARS COVERING THE LATTER PART OF THE 18TH CENTURY and generally up to the first half of the 19th century can be said to cover the period of art history known as the Romantic Era, although this is simplifying what is and has become a very blurred concept. A definition is equally difficult to establish, but loosely speaking Romanticism was more an attitude of mind rather than a clearly defined school of art, conveying an intensity of mood and feeling. It represented a need for artists, including composers and writers, to confront and overcome a hostile environment, but without coming to terms with it; to see the failings of the present, with its obsession with materialism, by looking back to the past with an increased sense of nostalgia; to identify in man's past achievements evidence and a recognition of man's inevitable fallibility, not as they were but as they are now, such as the ruins of some classical piece of architecture. One source has described Romanticism as a poetical view of society, which in itself is a Romantic definition, with its symbols represented by the ruin and the wreath. The general concept is indeed not restricted to this period, but is apparent today, albeit very much less widespread, with similar attitudes being expressed and a desire for aspects of the past which are invariably seen as a mental image completely out of context with the original reality.

Within the context of the above definition of Romanticism, it becomes difficult to identify marine painters who worked within its blurred parameters. This is partly because to paint the sea it is necessary to have an affinity and sympathy with it, especially if the aim is to capture a particular mood. It becomes even more difficult if ships are placed within this mood and are intended to become part of it. For this reason it is possible to recognize an underlying Romanticism in the works of artists before and after the period normally defined as encompassing this era. Charles Brooking (see Chapter Three) has often been considered to have anticipated the Romantic movements especially in marine painting. Although his battle scenes were intended to be accurate visual representations, some of Nicholas Pocock's work also conveys concepts which might be attributed to the Romantics.

The human element of a naval battle was invariably left to the imagination of the viewer in earlier marine paintings. The emphasis was on the position of the fleets in relation to each other, and although often accurate historical records, they could appear bland and repetitive, especially to those with a limited understanding of the sea. Two early and conscious attempts to reverse this and bring out the human tragedy of war at sea were made by the American-born artists John Singleton Copley and Benjamin West, although interestingly and possibly significantly too, neither was a specialist in marine painting.

COPLEY AND WEST

John Copley was born in Boston of Irish parents in 1738, and it was in Boston that he established himself as a portrait painter. However, for reasons of personal political beliefs, he left America, and in 1775 settled in England, where he developed an interest in historical subjects. His contribution to marine painting was through two famous canvases, *Watson and the Shark* (1778) and *The Siege and Relief of Gibraltar* (1783). Both are extremely dramatic in human terms, to the point of almost eliminating the marine element. The former, in the National Gallery of Art, Washington DC, with its emphasis on the men in the longboat trying to save the unfortunate Watson, who is on the verge of being attacked by a shark, lacks the calm and more moving human reality depicted by the marine artists of the late 19th and early 20th centuries. Copley was not concerned with absolute historical accuracy, even though this painting was commissioned by Watson himself. For a loosely defined marine painting, the expressions of the individuals – four of whom almost appear to be related, from the similarities in their looks – and the composition sum up the concept of the Romantic movement in painting. The second painting, in the Tate Gallery, London, also shows Copley's lack of concern for historical accuracy; it uses a well-documented event as a vehicle for Copley's interest in man's struggle against his own kind. It also shows the artist's poor knowledge of ship design and construction. Copley died in 1816.

THE FRENCH SHIP-OF-THE-LINE *COMMERCE DE PARIS* , 1804
Ange-Joseph Antoine Roux (1765–1835)
Peabody Museum of Salem

The combination of technical accuracy (which is of immense value to the maritime historian) and the aesthetic beauty of a well-drawn and rendered watercolour painting is characteristic of the work of this justifiably renowned French ship-portrait painter. However, it is sad to note that outside the USA little of his, or his children's and father's work, is reproduced. This is even more surprising when one remembers that a large collection remains hidden from view in the Musée de la Marine in Paris. This painting is from his middle period, for in later life he developed the technique of applying even finer detail to his finished works. This applies to both the vessels and the seas. Nevertheless, this is an outstanding example of his natural skills as a draughtsman, which he used to considerable effect.

Also born in 1738, but shortly after Copley, Benjamin West earned a living as a portrait painter and signwriter in Philadelphia. He travelled to Rome in 1759, which influenced his early style, and after winning favour with George III of England, settled in London, dying there in 1820.

West is particularly well known to marine art historians for his study of *The Battle of La Hogue*, executed in 1778. Hanging in the National Gallery of Art, Washington DC, it is a reconstruction of an incident during the five-day battle fought between the French and a combined Dutch and English fleet in 1692. Unlike Copley, West appears to have been determined to ensure historical and technical accuracy, for he visited the British fleet at Spithead to observe the effect of cannon-smoke. The admiral commanding ordered some of the vessels to manoeuvre and fire broadsides, enabling West to make notes on the effect, the most notable of which was the extent to which the smoke eliminated much of the natural light, which he later incorporated into his battle scene. The focal point of the painting is not so much the overall battle, but the hand-to-hand fighting taking place from longboats amid wreckage and struggling, water-sodden sailors, with the main battle as a backdrop. While there is almost a sense of amateur dramatics in the expressions of the men, West has managed to convey intensity of movement, with fear, complacency, aggression and serenity. The men-of-war visible show minor errors of technical accuracy, but in general they are more convincing than those drawn by Copley, and it may be safely assumed that West had access to the many drawings and paintings produced by the Van de Veldes on which to base his drawings of the vessels shown.

The work of both Copley and West should be seen as contributing to the development and progression of the Romantic movement generally and not in terms of marine painting specifically, except as a minor branch of it which did not have any great influence. Their place in the history of art must of course be recognized, but they are of little consequence in marine painting except to show how other artists used events at sea to extend their concern for and awareness of a hostile environment, whether man-made or created by the instincts of nature.

GÉRICAULT

However, if one looks beyond the genre of marine painting and includes other aspects of painting in general, it becomes clear that the French achieved the purest development in Romanticism, a noteworthy example being Jean Louis André Théodore Géricault (1791–1824), who is hailed as one of the founders of French Romanticism. Although he was not a marine painter as such, the work for which he is most famous, *The Raft of the "Medusa"*, executed in 1817 after his return from Italy, is

THE FRENCH SHIP *L'ORIENT* BLOWING UP AT THE BATTLE OF THE NILE, 1798

George Arnald (1763–1841)

National Maritime Museum, London

Arnald is better known for his prolific output of landscape paintings; he only rarely executed marines, but when he did he was able to produce work of outstanding quality, and the painting reproduced here is no exception. It is also his most famous, and it is not difficult to see why, for the impact, tragedy and atmosphere contained in it is overpoweringly moving.

Antne Roux a Marseille 1804

marine or nautical in content. It is also one of the earliest paintings which show in detail an aspect of life at sea: the unfortunate – and macabrely rendered – risk of shipwreck. This painting was based on real events comprising a mixture of heroics, tragedy and politics, not to say horrendous human suffering including murder and cannibalism. With such ingredients, it appealed to Géricault's Romantic impulses.

TURNER AND CONSTABLE

Of course no inclusion of Romanticism and the Romantic Era can be made without reference to Joseph William Mallord Turner. Again, Turner, born in London in 1775, was predominantly a landscape painter, but he was equally competent in depicting the sea and ships. His ability was early recognized, and he had his first painting hung at the Royal Academy when he was only 15. The quality of his marine work, and indeed of many of his landscapes, varies considerably, depending very much on one's viewpoint and the visual impact of such material in relation to what one hopes to achieve when studying it. Personally, the present author finds much of his later work to be almost repetitive, as if based on what became a successful formula, leading Turner to develop the style almost to the point of overworking it. On the other hand, his earlier work shows his skill as a draughtsman and ability to observe accurately from life, even though at times he was prone to exaggerate the proportions of vessels – for example, in the watercolour *A First-Rate taking in Stores*, painted in 1818 and now in the Cecil Higgins Art Gallery, Bedford. A painting which has become famous worldwide – to some the most famous of all marine paintings – and synonymous with Turner's style is his *The Fighting "Téméraire" Tugged To Her Last Berth To Be Broken Up* (1838) in the National Gallery, London. This again shows Turner's deliberate distortion of the proportions of the old first-rate, which tends to detract from the historical accuracy of the image, but then it is highly unlikely that Turner was concerned with minor considerations such as this, which is why he is often termed a Romantic painter. Many of Turner's marine paintings from this period lack a certain conviction, but demonstrate his obsession with the effects of light and colour, of which his understanding is undoubtedly supreme. The increasingly abstract nature of his work has opened up a separate Turner industry of art criticism, which has kept numerous art historians busy for many years.

The real beauty of Turner's work lies in his sketchbooks, which in comparatively recent years have received a wider recognition, although still lacking in the attention they so obviously deserve. This is unfortunate for they clearly show the artist's aptitude for recording his environment in a manner devoid of contrived style or technique. This is a classic example of the difference between the artist's personal records, which are not intended for public showing, and the finished paintings, which contain elements of conformity to the trends and fashions of the day. It confirms that studies of marine artists' work should always include substantial examples of their sketches and preparatory drawing, though this is often impossible as such sketches are either not available or considered of only secondary importance, when the opposite may well be true. They can in fact be quite as beautiful and inspiring as the highly finished and sometimes laboured paintings.

Specific examples of Turner's sketchbook studies constitute the basis of the books by Gerald Wilkinson, of which one of the most outstanding covers Turner's early years between the ages of 14 and 27, *Turner's Early Sketchbooks*. Although the original sketchbooks contain earlier examples of drawings and watercolours of marine subjects, the earliest reproduced in this book was completed when Turner was aged 20. One year later he was continuing to observe accurately and with conviction, combining his drawing skill with a clear understanding and application of colour, resulting in sketches with a limited but controlled palette. Two particular examples show that Turner's powers included an ability to convey accurately how ships were constructed without unnecessary detail. They are a sketch of a Thames sailing barge and a study of a full-rigged ship. Each has a beauty and level of artistic achievement which Turner was eventually to lose in his much later impressionistic paintings.

Turner has often been referred to as the greatest genius of British painting, and while this may have some substance in painting as a whole, there is an underlying feeling that his prolific output during a long and successful career – he died in 1851 at the age of 76 – has contributed primarily to this belief, but quantity is no substitute for quality and never should be. Furthermore, the honour of genius does not apply within the field of marine painting, for there have been many both before and after Turner who have not only contributed more to the genre, but have achieved a greater understanding of it.

The equally famous landscape painter John Constable (1776–1837) was another from this period (although only on the periphery of what is defined by Romanticism), who undertook a number of marine paintings and watercolours. Even though he appears to have had an abhorrence of the sea, some of his most beautiful work was the result of an extended coastal voyage he made in 1803. During this voyage he produced numerous sketches, executed primarily in pencil with grey washes, which are reminiscent of the Van de Veldes, showing an almost comparably spontaneous and lively approach. However, Constable's oil paintings of marine subjects have the same heavily laboured finish which he so painstakingly incorporated into his landscapes and for which he has become an almost household name, even among those who have no interest in painting.

THE NEEDLES
John Sell Cotman (1782–1842)
City of Norwich Museums
Cotman was one of the greatest exponents of the English School of watercolour painting, and his work contrasts well with the technique adopted by the Roux family.

◁ THE AMERICAN SHIP *ULYSSES*, 1798
Ange-Joseph Antoine Roux (1765–1835)
Peabody Museum of Salem
Ange-Joseph Roux is known to have painted at least three watercolours of this American-owned vessel and this is undoubtedly the best of them.

▷ THE FRENCH SHIP OF THE LINE *LE WAGRAM*
Ange-Joseph Antoine Roux (1765–1835)
Peabody Museum of Salem
Another superb example of this artist's work, showing the ship at anchor, drying her sails and with her decks full of activity. It is again both informative and pleasing.

LOUTHERBOURG

It is necessary to mention at this point a particularly important painter who may be said to epitomize the concepts of Romanticism combined with the exactitude of marine painting – the Frenchman Philippe-Jacques de Loutherbourg (1740–1812). Born in Strasbourg, he studied under his father, but received a thorough grounding in painting from the marine painter Francesco Casanova (1727–1802). Loutherbourg had already achieved a not inconsiderable degree of success in France when he moved to London in 1771. Essentially a landscape painter concerned very much with the recreation of dramatic, naturalistic light effects in a strong Romantic tradition, he limited his marine work to a number of distinguished naval scenes, the most notable of which is his large canvas *The Battle of the Glorious First of June, 1794*, in the National Maritime Museum, Greenwich. This painting almost defies description for there is so much activity, movement and drama contained within it. It is a painting which refuses to stay still. From where Loutherbourg acquired his knowledge of naval vessels is not known, but in this painting there is an accuracy which does not suggest it was drawn by an uninformed but keen amateur. His ships, their sails and rigging have a solidity and reality to them which is almost three-dimensional, and whatever reference source he used for the ships, there can be no doubt that he had a natural and highly developed ability.

In many respects the quality of Loutherbourg's marine work exceeds that of Turner's, and we may note that Turner was influenced by the Frenchman and admired his work greatly. It is a pity Loutherbourg did not concentrate more on marine studies, for it would have been interesting to see how much more he would have developed. But what few pieces he did complete are worth extended examination.

JOHN SELL COTMAN

With the exception of some of the artists mentioned above, and others who painted marine subjects but did not specialize in them, notably the German Caspar David Friedrich (1774–1840), the Romantic movement did not have such a profound effect on marine painting as it did on other areas of the arts. Naturally it is possible to identify the influence in the work of some, but it was predominantly through landscape and historical subjects that Romanticism can be said to have reached its more developed expression. This should be remembered when considering this period and the marine paintings emanating from it, because it is not as clearly defined as the title of this chapter may suggest. Furthermore, we are not concerned solely with those whose work is part of Romanticism as such, but also with those belonging to the Romantic Era.

In this context, it is appropriate to highlight the extraordinary level of achievement reached by English watercolour painters through the work of one particular individual, a contemporary of both Turner and Constable, John Sell Cotman, who, with Thomas Girtin (1775–1802) among others, epitomizes the great English School of watercolour painting. Cotman was born in Norfolk in 1782. Although his drawing ability was recognized at school, it appears he had no formal training. Nevertheless, at the age of 16 he left home for London to set himself up as an artist, but in 1806 returned to his beloved Norfolk where he died in 1842. Cotman worked exclusively in watercolours and, although chiefly a landscape painter, he did produce some memorable marine studies which to this day appear as fresh as if the paint had dried only minutes before. He was also not unfamiliar with the sea, for he owned a small sailing-boat which he used extensively to explore the river Thames and the east coast of England.

His work is stylized to some extent, for Cotman was concerned with the interpretation of nature, its moods and many variations of light through broad washes of transparent watercolour, rather than technical accuracy, even though he was capable of the latter, for he had a natural eye when it came to observation drawing. His ability to control washes and to create just the right balance in both tone and colour juxtaposition creates in the observer's mind detail which does not exist, but which is apparent because the subconscious mind has previously registered it. This is not to suggest that Cotman was in any way a forerunner of the Impressionists, but that he was a great and highly skilled exponent of the traditional use of watercolour.

There are four marine watercolours which will always be associated with Cotman's style and approach; they are *The "Mars" riding at anchor off Cromer*, (*c.*1807), *The Needles*, *Yarmouth River* (*c.*1809) and *A Dismasted Brig* (*c.*1808). The first two are in the City of Norwich Museums and the other two in the British Museum in London. It is interesting to compare these with the work of other contemporary marine watercolour painters, such as the French Roux family, and of modern marine painters. Cotman stands alone in using the medium as he did with strong, gradated and flat washes, while others used and continue to use the medium either as colouring to be applied over a finely detailed pencil drawing, or with the degree of finish usually associated with oil painting. And of course one is not better or more acceptable than the other, for it all depends very much on what the artist is hoping to achieve and what he wishes to convey to the viewer.

Unlike many of his contemporary marine painters, Cotman's work shows none of the influence of the Dutch. It is peculiarly English in all aspects, and reflects a separate line of development founded in the English landscape watercolour painters of the 17th and 18th centuries.

To reflect on the beauty and tranquillity of many of the paintings which were produced through the distinctive English school of watercolour painting is almost to separate the lives of the artists from the international turmoils through which they lived. This period saw the independence of the British colonies in North America and with it an increase in trade between the states on both sides of the Atlantic, as well as the Mediterranean, not forgetting the almost permanent state of war as one nation tried to enforce its supremacy on another, or gain for itself new colonies. The paradox which this creates to our late-20th century minds is striking until one considers that even though nations were expanding at an incredible rate, the lack of speed in communication meant enforced isolation from the many wars and battles. For most individuals, their involvement in national events was limited.

JOSEPH AND ANGE-JOSEPH ROUX

As the sea was the major means of communication and trade, extensive employment was to be found by those with even a limited level of skill if they lived in the vicinity of a major port. The science and art of navigation was constantly being improved and advanced upon and there was a corresponding requirement for charts and navigational instruments. In the French port of Marseilles a young man set himself up in business as a hydrographer, supplying the needs of many French and foreign captains. More influential than this business was the dynasty of marine painters which he unwittingly founded, and which remained active for well over 100 years, producing works which not only provide us with an accurate record of the appearance, design and construction of merchant, naval and native Mediterranean vessels, but are also beautiful and outstanding examples of the marine painter's art. The man in question was Joseph Roux, born in Marseilles in 1725.

Because he concentrated on working on the success of his hydrography business, Joseph Roux was not as prolific a marine painter as his son and grandchildren were to be, although he nevertheless developed a convincing style in both oils and watercolours, concentrating on naval events and ship portraits. From surviving examples of his work he would appear to have been self-taught, and although he had access to the ships he portrayed for reference purposes, his ability to depict a ship accurately in its natural environment was not as advanced as it might have been. They have a decidedly amateurish appearance. The Peabody Museum of Salem, Massachusetts, USA, holds two of his oil paintings, both executed in the early 1780s. Joseph Roux died in 1793.

Joseph's son, Ange-Joseph Antoine (sometimes listed as Joseph-Ange), was born in Marseilles in 1765. He quickly acquired an understanding of his father's business and with it a knowledge of ship design, construction and rig, as well as the manner by which ships were sailed, possibly and very likely from practical experience. Little evidence survives as to how and by whom he was taught to draw and paint, but there can be no doubt that he was influenced by his father. The tight and rigid draughtsmanship required in the preparation of charts must have also contributed to his artistic and drawing development. An early sketchbook by Ange-Joseph in the Peabody Museum of Salem, dated 1790, shows how competent he was by the age of 25. Here is evidence of an artist who was able to observe accurately from life and record it with a confident pencil line, without the need to conceal drawing errors by covering the sketches with excessive and unnecessary shading. Others demonstrate his ability to handle washes of transparent watercolour with an equal conviction, resulting in working sketches which to many modern artists would constitute a finished painting. Other sketchbooks from later periods show no diminution of artistic ability, but rather an enhancement of what was undeniably a natural gift, rather than an acquired skill. Whether he was observing and drawing a vessel, the harbour mouth, a ship on the stocks, a group of fishermen or shipwrights at work, his sketches always reflect a strong sense of reality and offer a visual explanation of many aspects of life associated directly or otherwise with the sea which is lacking in many marine artists' work, then and now.

As with many marine artists whose sketchbooks and preparatory drawings have survived, those by Ange-Joseph Antoine Roux should be more widely reproduced to enable a greater understanding of historical marine observation drawing to be acquired and appreciated. Sadly, they remain committed to the depths of museum archives, only rarely seeing the light of day, and then only to a privileged few. Part of the reason for this is the lesser importance attached to marine painting and illustration in comparison with other art forms, and the inevitable insignificance attached to so many marine artists' work. But when one considers the importance both then and now of the sea as a means of transportation, it is surprising that this should be the case.

Ange-Joseph Roux was able to maintain and transfer the fresh and spontaneous quality of his sketches into his more highly finished paintings, the majority of which were produced in transparent and opaque watercolour, sometimes over black, grey or sepia ink holding lines. These holding lines were applied only on the vessels; the seas, skies and, if appropriate, harbour mouths and other visible architectural detail relying only on the variations in colour and tone to separate them. In other cases, linear details on the hulls and rigging were picked out with a fine brush after the base washes had been applied. This contrast in technique gave the ships a crispness heightened by the amount of detail incorporated into them, which has become a very distinctive hallmark in the watercolours of all members of the Roux family. In fact it is a technique which can be identified in the work of other French marine painters from the same location and at about the same period, for example in the work of Michel-Félice Corne (*c.*1762–1832). Whether ink was used or not, Ange-Joseph always prepared an accurate and carefully executed pencil drawing, including at this stage as much detail as possible.

Unlike many of the English exponents of watercolour painting, the Roux family rarely used a heavily textured paper, relying very much on what is referred to as a Hot Pressed paper and also a laid paper, such as Ingres paper. This smoothness of paper allowed for the sail and rigging detail to be faithfully reproduced with fine, consistent lines, but did not allow for a very wet and broad treatment to be used on the seas or sky, which is often considered the traditional use of the medium. Nevertheless, the fact that seas and skies had to be broken down into almost geometrical shapes with the distinctive, but subtle pattern created by flat and gradated washes drying on a comparatively smooth paper did not hinder Ange-Joseph, and he used them to great effect. And the surface texture did not prevent him from producing some imaginative, but realistically convincing skies.

Much of the work of Ange-Joseph has found its way into the extensive collection of marine paintings and drawings in the Peabody Museum of Salem. The Museum has published three excellent books wherein one may study the work of the Roux family to a greater extent. These are the official catalogues, *Marine Paintings and Drawings in the Peabody Museum* (1968), and *More Marine Paintings and Drawings in the Peabody Museum* (1979). The final book is a catalogue devoted to the complete collection of Roux paintings, drawings and sketchbooks, *The Artful Roux: Marine Painters of Marseille* (1978).

It may be asked why so much of this family's work has found its way to the USA. At the time that Joseph and Ange-Joseph Antoine Roux were practising as both hydrographers and marine painters, there was an increasing demand for accurate ship portraits. This demand was not restricted to the Mediterranean area, but was becoming widespread as ships extended their sphere of operations and the owners and captains wished to have either a record of their ship for its own sake, or a record of their ship entering or leaving a particular foreign port. America was not slow in expanding its trading links abroad, and as a consequence the captains of her merchant ships took back with them many paintings by European artists. As the Roux family's style is so distinctive, so their association with the USA seems more pronounced than it does with the country of their birth where they all permanently resided, although the largest collection of Roux paintings

THE *GOREE* IN ACTION WITH THE *PALINURE* AND THE *PILADE* , OFF MARIE GALANTE
Thomas Luny (1759–1837)
Royal Exchange Gallery, London
Executed in 1815, this oil painting typifies the style of this well-known marine artist. Even though invalided out of the Navy about 1808, and eventually confined to a wheelchair with his disability affecting his hands, he managed to produce an almost incredible number of paintings without any serious or noticeable decline in quality.

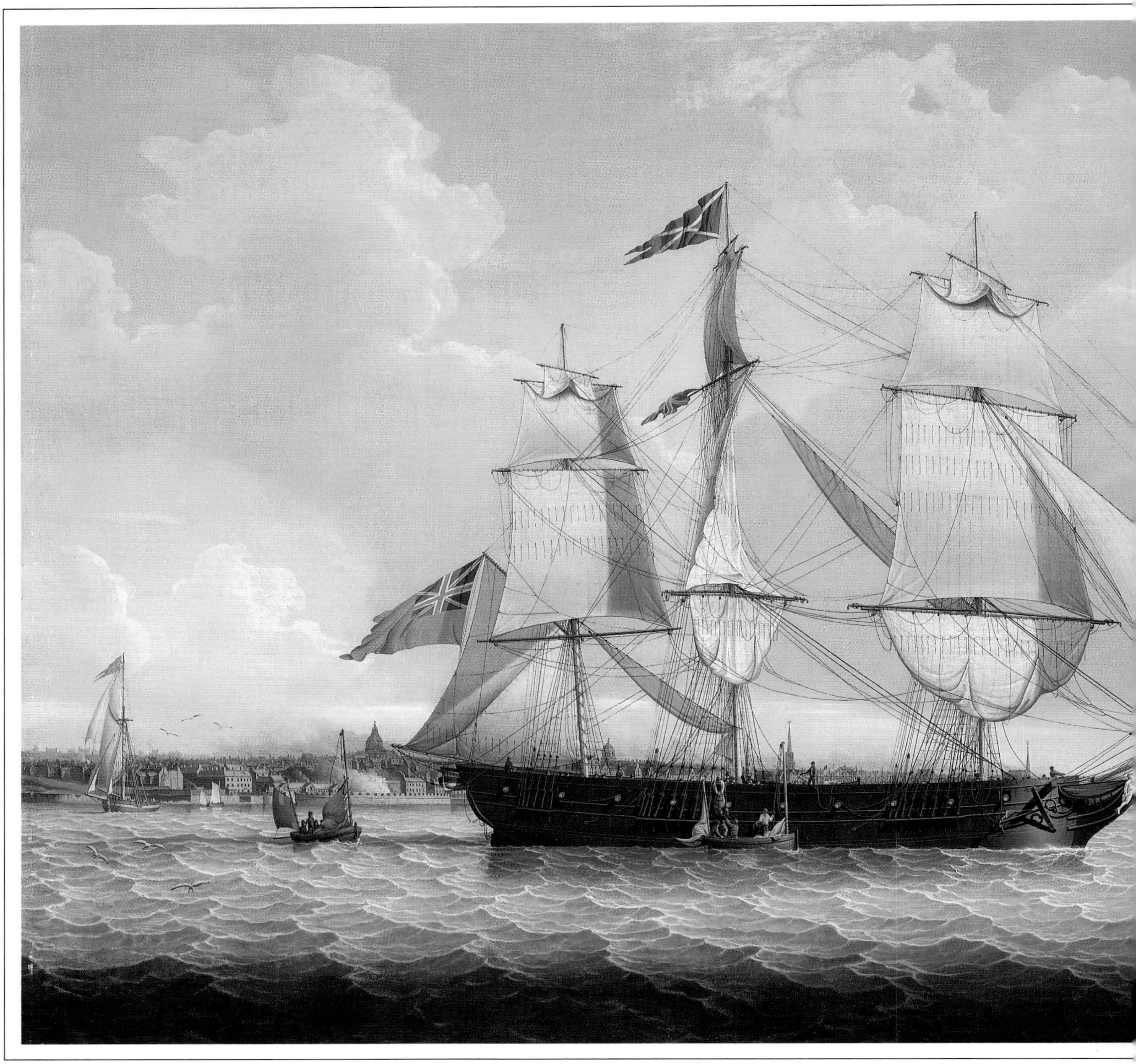

A MERCHANTMAN BELONGING TO THE JARDINE MATHESON LINE WITH OTHER SHIPPING OFF LIVERPOOL
Robert Salmon (1775–*c.* 1845)
Christie's, London

Salmon was one of those marine artists who were prolific as ship-portrait painters in both England and America; this example is representative of his English work. Although his life also spanned the Romantic Era, he was not influenced by it, but preferred to concentrate on what he undoubtedly excelled at – the accurate and seamanlike rendering of ships, often in a harbour-mouth or river setting. The detail in this example is typical and worth considerable study. The accuracy is enhanced by Salmon's excellent control of his chosen medium as well as his understanding of natural light conditions.

is in fact in the Musée de la Marine in Paris.

It is stated that there was much competition between captains, owners and merchants to secure Ange-Joseph's services in illustrating their vessels, which has resulted in his works being found in many national collections all over the world – although it was still with some surprise that this author came across his first original Roux in the Norsk Sjøfartsmuseum in Oslo some years ago. Roux eventually died as a result of an attack of cholera in Marseilles in 1835 at the age of 70. Records suggest that he never retired from his business or from his paintings.

Through his marriage to Rose Catelin, Ange-Joseph Antoine Roux had four children, three boys and one girl, each of whom was to become a marine watercolour painter, the boys also entering their father's hydrography business. Although each was active during the period covered by this chapter, they represent just one small link between the marine painters of the early 19th century and those of the latter half, and will therefore be described in Chapter Five, which deals generally with the 19th century.

This chapter, while confining itself loosely to a clearly defined period, has demonstrated the diversity of styles and approaches adopted by marine painters. It has shown how some were permitted the luxury of being able to develop without an immediate concern for making a living, through previous successes, while others developed a style or technique which appealed to a particular clientele concerned more with technical accuracy than artistic impressionism. In so doing, it re-emphasizes the difficulty in placing marine artists into particular schools or movements. The study of the progression from one generation of artists to another is necessary and important, but it does not supersede the basic and underlying need to study and understand the work of individual artists on their own merits and not constantly in comparison with others, when a comparison is not always valid or justifiable.

CHAPTER FIVE

The 19th Century in Europe and the USA
1800–1900

WE HAVE NOW REACHED A STAGE WHERE WE CAN DISCUSS the 19th century proper, but in the developments discussed in Chapters Three and Four the early part of this extremely important century, as far as marine painting is concerned, has already been touched upon. This is unavoidable, simply because unlike so many other areas of art history, with the possible and notable exception of the Dutch School, the history and development of marine painting does not readily conform to parameters or norms. Also, marine painting is, and continues to be, a less dominant art form, which makes it difficult to slot particular periods or artists into schools or movements. In marine painting this creates an extensive overlap between the periods nominally covered here, because of the style of an individual artist's work or, more fundamentally and even less to do with art history, because of the years covered by their lives, the immediate environment in which they practised and the external influences with which they came into contact.

Marine painters like Nicholas Pocock were active during some of the period covered by the Romantic Era, but in relation to much of what Romanticism was about, were either not influenced by it or did not subscribe to the intangible notions it generated, while they continued developing their own style and technique. This is also true of the two Roux discussed so far, even though they have been included in the chapter dealing with the Romantic Era. They are therefore seen quite correctly as being separate from Romanticism. This illustrates the difficulty of discussing as specific an art form as marine painting in strict chronological order and in terms of strict definitions.

It is always advisable, partly for the reasons mentioned, to study marine painting by first examining the quality of an individual's work and what he intended to achieve, if anything more than a mere desire to record contemporary or historic events or even the sea itself as something worthy of translating onto paper or canvas. Such a study should be followed by assessing the developments which influenced him. Admittedly, this will tend to develop into a very subjective attitude on the part of the student, but being governed by one's personal preferences is infinitely preferable to being dictated to by many art historians, who tend to dismiss marine painting out of hand and without just cause.

CLARKSON STANFIELD

Regardless of current opinion of marine painting by art historians, the century being discussed in this chapter recognized the genre as being relevant and of equal importance to any other art form, which obviously went some way in encouraging young artists to take up marine painting professionally with a reasonable chance, if they were of above average ability, of making a living from it. One British artist who did take up marine painting professionally and succeed in making a name for himself during his own lifetime, and has since come to represent all that was excellent about the subject in the first half of the century, was Clarkson Stanfield.

Born in 1793 in what was then a small town, but was already starting to expand into what eventually became one of the world's greatest shipbuilding towns, Sunderland on the River Wear, on the north-eastern coast of England, he was the son of an Irish actor and author who had settled in the town to run a wine and spirit business. Stanfield's early years included child parts on the stage, until at the age of 12 he was apprenticed to a heraldic painter in Edinburgh. This proved unsatisfactory and he ran away to sea in 1808, after having served only two years of the apprenticeship. Following a number of voyages in merchant ships he was impressed into the Royal Navy and drafted to HMS *Namur*, where his natural artistic talent came to the fore when he painted the scenery for a play put on by the crew. Bad health terminated his naval career and he was discharged in 1814, although he returned to sea a year later as a seaman on board the East Indiaman *Warley*, bound for China. Completing the round voyage and discharging in London, Stanfield took up employment as a scene painter in an East London theatre before spending a brief time doing the same in Edinburgh. He returned to London, and by 1822 his stage sets at Drury Lane began earning him a not inconsiderable reputation.

DUTCH PINKS AT SCHEVENINGEN, 1860
Edward William Cooke (1811–80)
Guildhall Art Gallery, London

Although known primarily for the numerous engravings he produced for his *Shipping and Craft,* which was published in 1828, Cooke was very much a product of the 19th-century English School of marine painting and owed much to the traditions and standards set by the great Dutch marine artists in the 17th century. Indeed, not only did Cooke study the work of these artists, but he also travelled to Holland on numerous occasions, especially to the long, exposed beaches at Scheveningen. He made many studies of the work of the local fishermen and the way in which they handled their boats, in all weather and sea conditions. The environment and activity obviously inspired him greatly, for he produced some highly memorable paintings, of which this is representative. When studying this painting, one soon becomes aware how knowledgeable Cooke was about the design, structure and rig of the vessels he drew. This painting, as well as demonstrating the artist's natural and highly skilled draughtsmanship, is beautifully observed, and it is particularly in the small detail that one begins to appreciate Cooke's marvellous understanding. This also applies to the way in which he has recorded the variations in light, shade and colour in all aspects of the painting.

During his time as a scene painter and scenic director Stanfield was also practising as a more traditional easel painter, and this activity soon began to take precedence in his life, to the point that by 1834 he was receiving sufficient commissions to be able to retire from his theatre work. However, before taking up painting professionally he had had his first work accepted by the Royal Academy in 1827, being elected an Associate Royal Academician in 1831, and even earlier by the comparatively newly formed Society of British Artists in 1823, achieving the Presidency of this society by 1829. By 1847 Stanfield had moved himself and his large family into a spacious house in Hampstead, north-west London, where he continued painting and was able to receive his increasingly large circle of distinguished artistic and literary friends. He continued to build on his reputation, and his last work to be hung at the Royal Academy was displayed to the public in the same month, May 1867, in which he died at the age of 74.

Clarkson Stanfield was considered by John Ruskin (1819–1900) that great, influential but sometimes extremely subjective and biased Victorian art critic and theorist, to be the nearest rival to Joseph Mallord William Turner. This was praise indeed and thoroughly justified, but if the comparison is made purely within the terms and definitions of marine painting, it could be said that Stanfield had in fact the edge on Turner. When the later works of both artists are examined, a great similarity is found between some of Stanfield's later works and Turner's earlier ones. Stanfield used his sea experience to excellent effect, producing dramatic and powerful compositions in both oils and watercolours, and his ships are always closely observed with a strong feeling of solidity about them. He did not restrict himself solely to marine subjects, but included landscapes and topographical subjects in his repertoire.

The Norwich and Hull Schools

In addition to the broad-based marine artists centred in and around London, the early part of this century saw develop in England two fairly distinctive regional schools of painting which had close associations with marine painting. One has become internationally renowned for the highly expressive manner in which watercolours were applied, even though the artists considered to have belonged to the school painted in both watercolours and oils. This was the Norwich School, effectively founded by the English landscape painter John Crome (1768–1821) in 1803 through his Norwich Society. The watercolourist John Sell Cotman, introduced in Chapter Four, and Crome himself have together and in particular given the Norwich School the status it so richly deserves in the history of English painting. The overwhelming majority of the work produced by artists from this school is of landscapes, but,

SPITHEAD

Edward Duncan (1803–82)

Birmingham Museums and Art Gallery

This painting has come to represent all that is excellent about this comparatively little-known artist, and no apology is needed for its inclusion here, because it must surely rank as one of the outstanding – and, indeed, inspiring – examples of English 19th-century marine watercolour paintings. It demonstrates what has become a very English tradition in the application of clean, transparent washes using a limited colour range, an aspect which has seen an unfortunate decline in standards in recent years. It is also carefully composed and, for all its apparent simplicity, well drawn.

WHALERS *SWAN* AND *ISABELLA* IN THE ARCTIC REGIONS
John Ward (1798–1849)
This is an excellent example of Ward's approach to marine painting combining accurate and detailed ship portraits with a setting in the ship's natural working environment. With his particular technique, it makes for a pleasing work of art as well as an important and informative historical record.

when they turned their attention to marine subjects they did so with an equal degree of sensitivity and observation.

Generally more isolated, and less well recognized as a separate school, was that established in the late 18th century in the Kingston-upon-Hull region, on the east coast of England – the Hull School. The importance of this increasingly thriving and productive port involved in the fishing and whale industries produced a number of talented artists, concerned primarily with the accurate recording of ships and the environment in which they operated. Probably the most famous and highly regarded artists from this school was John Ward, who not only was born in Hull in 1798, but spent his entire life there until he died of cholera at the age of 51 in 1849. His knowledge of ships came from his father, who was a master of a small coastal brig, while his training as an artist resulted from his apprenticeship to a house and ship painter.

For some unusual but very welcome reason, John Ward's marine paintings are possibly seen by more people than those of many of his more internationally famous counterparts, because they are frequently reproduced on greeting cards, in particular his serene and appealing *The Return of the "William Lee"*, painted *c.*1839 and considered one of his best works. This painting is undeniably excellent, but there are others which are comparable, if not in some respects better, such as his moderately sized painting *Hull Whalers in the Arctic*, in the collection of Hull Museums. Although slightly marred by the poorly drawn polar bear in the foreground, this painting has a balanced composition and contains five whalers, the three immediately to view being carefully observed and drawn down to the smallest of detail, clearly showing Ward's depth of knowledge about the ships from his home town.

MAN-OF-WAR OFF MOUNT EDGECUMBE, 1839
Nicholas Matthews Condy the Younger (1818–51)
N.R. Omell Galleries, London
While in no way an inferior marine artist, Condy does not rank among the more notable; his work conforms very much with and is typical of the middle range of marine paintings from the first half of the century. This small oil on board is carefully composed but lacks the finish of some of his larger works.

The number of accurate paintings Ward completed of whalers and the Arctic has led to a belief that he made at least one trip with the fleet to record the industry first-hand. This may indeed be true, but it is not supported by the accuracy of his ships alone, for he could just as well have drawn them at Hull. What would be more telling would be the frozen landscapes in which he placed his ships, and these tend to appear as if drawn and painted by impression rather than from life. John Ward is one of the many marine artists whose work reached a high level of maturity; his early death leads us to speculate as to what he might have achieved had he lived longer.

Both the Norwich and the Kingston-upon-Hull Schools were relatively short-lived in terms of those artists whose work can be related directly to their influences and techniques. By the second half of the century many of the artists based in these regions of England had either developed more independent styles or those which reflected the increased power, impact and atmosphere of the great age in which the artists found themselves.

Shipbuilding in Victorian Britain

The 19th century was dominated in Great Britain by the reign of Queen Victoria, who came to the throne in 1837, and gave her name to one of the great ages in the development of a nation. It was dominated by Britain's supremacy at sea, both in naval terms and through her vast merchant fleet, elements of which could be found in practically every country which wanted to buy or had something worthwhile to sell, even if the price was unfairly negotiated at times. In addition, Britain's industrial wealth and constantly growing Empire ensured her place at the forefront of all national and international

STE MARGUERITE , CAPTAIN JN JS CAUCHIE, CAPTURED 28 MAY 1803, PRISONER-OF-WAR IN ENGLAND UNTIL 3 SEPTEMBER 1812 AND EXCHANGED IN 1813

François Geoffroi Roux (1811–82)

Peabody Museum of Salem

This delightful example of François Roux's ship-portrait style, in watercolour, was painted in 1839, some time after the event described in the caption which forms the base of the painting. The detail is not only excellent but accurate as well, especially in the masts, spars, sails and rigging. In the last case, very little of either the standing or running rigging has been omitted; even the gaskets are shown on the two topsails. The crew figures too are positioned in accordance with the set of the sails and the brig's obvious and recent departure from port. The three in the bows are either securing the port anchor for sea, or getting ready to hoist the jib, and immediately aft of the fore mast, crew members are pulling home the sheets of the fore-topgallant sail. This close attention to detail is typical of the way in which the Roux family approached their work, and remains the principal reason why these ship portraits are such useful and important historical records. They are also extremely attractive marine paintings in their own right.

developments. The 19th century also saw greater technological developments at sea than any other century before and as it progressed, there was a gradual increase in the number of specialist marine painters. This testifies to the growing awareness of the importance of the sea in the development and expansion of industrialized and colonial powers, even though, as mentioned before, it still continued to be less widely practised than other art forms. However, in comparison to earlier periods marine painting was practised by more individuals and reached its peak in popularity during the course of the 19th century, and into the Edwardian Age. It can therefore be said to be the most exciting, especially in terms of the many powerful images which remain to inspire future generations. Because historical events so directly influenced the subject-matter of marine artists, and indeed the way in which some approached their work, it is necessary to outline briefly some of these profound changes at sea.

The average individual's life is only gradually affected by major technological changes, but for those whose lives were linked directly or otherwise with the sea in the 19th century, there were dramatic and fast-changing technological developments, even though improvements to basic living conditions did not change as quickly. In broad terms, the 19th century progressed from the realities of the wooden-built sailing warship engaging the enemy with the limited flexibility and range of broadside fire, as at Trafalgar in 1805, to the introduction in 1891 of the first turret warship, HMS *Hood*, whose main armament had a range of approximately 6.75 miles. Between 1805 and 1891 much else happened, with each event or development having a specific or broad-based impact on shipbuilding, marine engineering, naval tactics, commercial transportation and travel at sea, each allowing in varying degrees the more developed countries to expand their influence and territorial gains.

Although sail continued to have a strong foothold throughout the 19th century, with the introduction of steam-powered vessels there was a gradual and for many years almost imperceptible decline in the dependence on canvas and wind power to get from port to port. The first successful attempt to build an ocean-going steam vessel, albeit with paddles and sail-assisted, was the PS *Great Western*, designed and launched by the Victorian civil engineer Isambard Kingdom Brunel in 1837. This was followed by Brunel's even greater achievement, the iron-built, screw-propelled, five-masted SS *Great Britain*, which was launched in Bristol in 1843 and sailed for her maiden voyage to New York in 1845. The intense conservatism of the Admiralty meant that naval developments took rather longer, and it was not until 1860 that the Royal Navy launched its first ironclad, and iron-built, screw-propelled warship. Even then, its building was encouraged more in direct response to the assumed threat resulting from the French building of the *Gloire* in 1859 rather than out of the desire to apply any new advances in naval architecture. This was the full-rigged ship HMS *Warrior*, launched in London in 1860, which laid the foundation for the most imposing and, at times, majestic warships the world has ever seen.

As important as was the building of these three ships, in contrast to other events at sea during this period they did not attract the attention of more than a few marine artists. For the most part, those artists who did appreciate the contribution of these ships towards the advancement of naval architecture, and made visual records of them, were not in the top echelons of their profession. The notable exception to this was the highly competent marine lithographer Thomas Goldsworthy Dutton (*c.*1819–91), who made at least one beautiful and accurate study of both the SS *Great Britain* and HMS *Warrior* soon after their respective launches.

Regardless of these technological advances, the 1850s, 1860s and 1870s saw the epitome of what is possibly man's most beautiful of creations, the square-rigged merchant sailing ship. These were ships with awe-inspiring names such as the *Ariel* (1865), the *Cairngorm* (1853), the *Fiery Cross* (1855), the *Stornoway* (1850), the *Thermopylae* (1868), the *Titania* (1866) and many, many more which captured the imagination of a nation by their speed and beauty. As with many of man's achievements, the building of these outstandingly proportioned vessels had its foundation in the expediency of war.

With the comparative peace which came about in Europe following the French defeat at Waterloo by the British in 1815, in addition to the peace with America in 1816, a period of unprecedented expansion of international trade followed, and continued almost unabated until the start of the First World War in 1914. It was through the need to beat the blockades imposed by the British on American east coast ports during the Napoleonic Wars, principally in the Chesapeake Bay region, that a type of sailing vessel developed which introduced the word "clipper" into the English language. In the first instance it was associated with the vessel's port of origin, Baltimore – hence the "Baltimore clipper", although the word's association with sailing ships did not come into widespread use until 1830. However, the design and reputation of these vessels and the speed they were capable of attaining soon attracted the attention of the Europeans, in particular the French, who quickly applied the design concepts to their own vessels. The British were slower in accepting the changes, and it was not until the 1820s that they started building vessels designed specifically for speed and for specific trades, such as for the Post Office, the fruit and opium trades. Besides these, trade in general with China continued to be developed which, with the repeal of the East Indiamen's monopoly in 1834, increased competition, which in turn increased the need for faster ships.

SOLON, CAPTAIN GEORGE BUCKNAM. RECEIVING PILOT OFF HÂVRE 29 MAY 1847
François Joseph Frédéric Roux (1805–70)
Peabody Museum of Salem
The ship *Solon*, built in Maine in 1834, is shown with her main-topsail and main-topgallant sails aback as she lies hove-to in order to pick up the pilot approaching from under her stern. This watercolour painting is very carefully drawn and typifies the importance attached by the Roux family to achieving nautical accuracy in preference to artistic embellishment.

In the first 15 or so years of the second half of the 19th century this continuous process of improvement reached a peak with both the British and Americans. Unlike so many manufactured objects which surround us and which are taken for granted because we accept them as the norm, clipper ships were always identified as being something special and significant. They therefore attracted the attention of marine artists who not only saw them as a contemporary subject worthy of recording by way of paintings, but also, and in the appropriate setting, as a subject which, with its almost accidental beauty was of widespread appeal, and therefore possibly quite lucrative too. That this appreciation of clipper ships has not diminished is evidenced by the number of modern marine artists who continue to use them as a primary reference source for their work. Indeed, since the demise of the clipper ship – and the large deep-water merchant sailing ships which followed – it is unlikely that there have been many marine artists who have not succumbed at some stage in their career to the attraction and appeal of depicting them on paper or canvas.

THE ROUX FAMILY – THE NEXT GENERATION

The Roux family of marine painters was introduced in Chapter Four through the work of Joseph Roux and his son Ange-Joseph Antoine Roux, whose own children continued the family tradition as hydrographers and

THE FRENCH BARQUE *PARNASSE,* 1841
François Geoffroi Roux (1811–82)
Peabody Museum of Salem
This painting shows the *Parnasse* hove-to, either having just dropped off someone or about to pick someone up, possibly a sedated and unwilling seaman required to make up the crew numbers – a typical occurrence during the 19th century. As usual the detail is accurate, making for an informative painting, which still retains all the qualities of an excellent example of marine painting.

artists. The period during which Ange-Joseph's children were active almost coincides with the development of the clipper ship from the blockade runners of the Napoleonic Wars to the crack opium, tea and wool clippers of later years, although being based in Marseilles, with the exception of one son, they had little contact with many of the really fine-lined vessels, but more with the unsung general traders, which in reality were more numerous and important. A study of their combined work during this period therefore provides an interesting contrast with the glorification of the clipper ship as depicted by so many of the north European artists. Their work is also an interesting and historically very useful record of the design and appearance of ships which, without the client-base promoting paintings of such vessels, ordinarily would not have been considered as worthy subjects.

Ange-Joseph's first child, who was born in 1799, was named Mathieu-Antoine Roux. He eventually took over an uncle's hydrographic business not far from his father's shop. He was obviously influenced by the artistic work of his father, as his own work is in much the same style, although he was not as prolific as either his father or indeed his younger brothers, and is considered inferior to them in technique and ability. This is most apparent in the way in which the sails are handled, which can at times appear rather stiff and rigid. From the few examples which have survived and are available for examination, it would also appear that Antoine Roux Jr restricted himself to portraying the hulls of the vessels in an almost true side elevation, a broadside view, and only attempted the more visually pleasing three-quarter views for vessels in the background. This may have been due to a lack of confidence or a lack of ability in understanding the direction and shape the compound curves would take as soon as a vessel is turned to any angle other than that which is parallel to the eye. Antoine Roux Jr died in 1872, and unfortunately his son did not continue with the ship-portrait painting tradition.

The next child was a daughter, Ursule Josephine Roux, about whom very little is known other than the fact that she also painted marine subjects. The Peabody Museum of Salem, Massachusetts, holds one example, which gives the impression of having been painted for pleasure rather than profit, a typical activity for young ladies at that time.

François Joseph Frédéric Roux was born next, in 1805. There is no doubt that Frédéric Roux's work is superior to that of his older brother, and his competence enabled him to sell his watercolours from at least the age of 17. Frédéric appears to have been the only member of the family to have received any formal art training, although it is important to appreciate that this was after he had already taken up painting through the direct encouragement and influence of his father. The opportunity for this training came about when the well-known French painter Antoine-Charles Horace Vernet (1758–1835) and his painter son visited the shop, which led to Frédéric's being sent to the Vernets' Paris studio.

It was while Frédéric was in Paris that he received an important commission from Admiral Willaumez, who requested a series of watercolour paintings illustrating the ships on which the admiral had served or with which he had had some involvement. The majority of these are now with the Musée de la Marine in Paris and unfortunately are rarely displayed or reproduced. They would provide an ideal opportunity for a study of early 19th century French naval vessels combined with one on the work of an important marine watercolour artist. Around 1835, after some years in Paris, Frédéric moved to the Channel port of Le Havre, where he combined his painting with the running of a hydrographer's shop and where he was to spend the rest of his life, travelling abroad and returning to his place of birth on a number of occasions. He died in 1870 at the age of 65.

Frédéric Roux's talent as a watercolour artist is undeniable, as was his knowledge of the design, construction and rig of the ships which frequented the port from where he worked. Although the majority of his work was in the tradition of ship portraits, he at times varied the position of the ships from the conventional broadside view and also varied the state of the sea to include storm conditions, with vessels under reduced canvas or under jury-rig (a temporary rig) after having been dismasted. One of his more unusual studies, executed in 1867, is of a group of

THE *EMILIE,* NANTES, CAP VR LEPETIT, 1857
François Geoffroi Roux (1811–82)
Peabody Museum of Salem
The *Emilie* was built at Lorient in 1855 and she is shown here moving along in a gentle breeze, under practically a full spread of canvas. It is a seamanlike study of a typical and once numerous type of merchant sailing ship.

unnamed sailing warships under manoeuvre. Even though the composition is excellent, this watercolour reflects the accuracy demanded by professional sailors rather than the interpretative element normally associated with works of art (although what is or is not fine art is difficult to define). It shows in the immediate foreground a 20- or 22-gun brig from the port side and under reduced sail, cutting acróss the stern of a large two-decker which is hove-to and depicted from the port quarter. To the right and in the middle distance is another two-decker heeling under a full spread of canvas on the starboard tack, while in the background and offset to the left, but in front of the ship which is hove-to, is a frigate, also close-hauled on the starboard tack.

Of particular interest, and often ignored in the study of marine painting, are Frédéric's sketchbooks, which have survived and which have over the years been purchased or donated and now reside in the Peabody Museum. The positive marks he made show little evidence of correction or error in the proportions. Traditional watercolour painting allows little room for error at the painting stage, and indeed excessive errors and corrections at the drawing stage are often apparent because of the transparent nature of the paint. Accurate and careful draughtsmanship is essential, especially when depicting ships, and so it is sometimes possible to judge an artist's skill in drawing by close study of the finished painting. Nevertheless, the freedom and spontaneity of an artist's private sketchbooks often reveals a great deal about his real drawing abilities. Unfortunately it is not always possible to see them on general public display in the national collections, but they are worth the study if they can be seen by appointment.

The last member of the Roux dynasty of marine painters was François Geoffroi Roux, born in 1811, who, like his two brothers and sister before him, was taught the rudiments of drawing and painting by his father. His work is generally more lively and the compositions more imaginative than those of the rest of the family, with no diminution in any way of the distinctive Roux attention to accuracy and detail. Like Frédéric, François achieved distinction with his marine paintings, including the *Palmes d'Officier d'Académie* (*des Beaux Arts*) and the Croix de la Légion d'Honneur. His most significant contribution to the development of French marine painting and the study of French naval architecture was a series of paintings he produced during a period spanning almost 20 years, showing French naval and merchant vessels from the last decade of the 18th century. He left them to the Louvre in Paris, where some remain to this day, although the Musée de la Marine own quite a number as well. Except for a few being reproduced in one of Admiral Paris's books published in 1885, this remarkable series is little known, which could explain why the work of the Roux family in general and François's in particular has not received sufficient attention to warrant their being considered great or important marine artists. As with so many marine artists' work, its value extends far beyond that of visually pleasing pictures, and is also of immense value to naval and maritime historians.

François Geoffroi Roux died in Marseilles in 1882, and even though the family line continues to this day, the more recent generations have not produced any further naturally talented marine artists. It can only be hoped that in the not too distant future one of the major French museums will give serious consideration to the publication of a definitive and well-illustrated study of the works of this distinguished family of artists.

Interpretations of Trafalgar

While the Roux concentrated on the humble merchant ship and occasional warship, the use of the clipper ship as a popular subject for marine artists was and is closely followed by those who have been inspired by Nelson's great victory against the combined French and Spanish fleets off Cape Trafalgar on 21 October 1805. Not only did this important naval victory inspire many of the leading marine artists of the day, but it continued to do so throughout the 19th century and indeed to this day. It would be well-nigh impossible to make a comprehensive study of the clipper ship in marine painting, but would not be so in respect of the battle of Trafalgar, and could include both the level of historical accuracy and the influence of written accounts on the artists. The use of acceptable artistic licence as demonstrated by Turner's two principal studies, compared with the use of the participating warships' logbooks and authenticated accounts by survivors by William Lionel Wyllie in his panoramic view at the Royal Navy Museum in Portsmouth, gives the impression that one has looked at paintings of two separate battles, although both explain clearly the respective artists' intentions. A more realistic comparison might be between Turner and Nicholas Pocock, as both were practising artists at the time the battle took place, but again there are extreme differences, with each painting reflecting the artists' interpretations and, more importantly, their influences. Turner, in his oil painting of 1806, is attempting to convey his personal impression of the human struggle and the overpowering proximity of the ships surrounding Nelson's flagship, the *Victory*, while Pocock's oils and watercolours clearly represent the no-nonsense approach of a former seaman to the recording of history.

Another artist who approached this battle with the seaman's eye but produced yet another interpretation was Clarkson Stanfield whose career has been outlined here. The Tate Gallery has his oil sketch for the large painting which he completed and which now hangs in the Institute of Directors' headquarters in London. These were painted

THE *BREILLE,* ON THE MAAS, HOLLAND
Pieter Cornelis Dommersen (flourished late 19th century)
Royal Exchange Art Gallery, London

Little is known about this Dutch marine artist, who appears to have been active during the latter half of the century, with some evidence existing which would indicate that he worked into the 20th century. He exhibited at the Royal Academy in 1865. The example reproduced appears to be typical of his oils, even though it is not as highly finished as others which have survived. It is a lively and competent study of a brig hove-to with a boat rowing out to meet her. Of particular note is the carefully observed effect of strong light against the darkness of the fast approaching gale. This balance of light and shadow, the clear emphasis and feeling of increasing wind speed and the already short sea being whipped up, combine to bring the whole composition to life. Dommersen was obviously very familiar with the environment he chose to paint, and although the brig is not as detailed as a Roux, there is sufficient detail to suggest he understood ships. The painting is very much in the tradition of the Dutch masters from the 17th century.

in 1833 and 1836 respectively. Stanfield has attempted to be very specific in the timing of his painting, having chosen the moment soon after Nelson was wounded at 2.30 in the afternoon. The ships are drawn with Stanfield's usual accuracy but, interestingly, those in the sketch are more convincing and sit more acceptably in the water, while those in the finished painting appear almost too delicate and top-heavy with their large and over-towering masts – a rare mistake for Stanfield to make. Unlike many of his other marine paintings, these have an unusual atmosphere about them, which could be the result of the very localized light and the glassy swell running, reflecting, mirror-like, the bows of the *Victory*, which have also been illuminated by the limited light. This major painting is not one of Stanfield's most successful paintings, but is often considered more favourably than Turner's other version of the battle, painted in 1823, because the latter lacks the nautical realism and accuracy of Stanfield's. Turner's was also not very popular with seamen, including King William IV.

A work by Daniel Maclise is in almost complete contrast to other treatments of the Battle of Trafalgar. Maclise, better known as a caricaturist and painter of historical and literary themes, was born in Ireland in 1806, and once he had moved to London quickly gained considerable popularity for his anecdotal canvases. In the early 1860s he was commissioned to paint two vast frescoes for the new Houses of Parliament, one of which was an almost lifesize impression of the deck of the *Victory* during the height of the battle. Entitled *The Death of Nelson*, it shows in the centre Nelson mortally wounded, surrounded by a seething mass of sailors and marines, with only superficial information to suggest that the incident took place at sea, which may be either a reflection on Maclise's lack of knowledge of ships or part of the terms of the commission. Unfortunately the composition lacks depth, and the incident appears to be confined to a long and narrow strip of deck, even taking into account the comparative lack of beam of the *Victory* herself and the fact that the port side of the ship is where the picture plane is located. Having said that though, the detail is superb and shows the artist's skill in rendering the human figure. Although Maclise no doubt could have had access to the ship if he so wished, the painting itself is predominantly fictional, for it would have been impossible to verify the positions of individual crew members at the time Nelson was shot. Nevertheless, it is a most impressive painting, full of movement and action. This painting took over two years of almost continuous work, and the demands of this and the other commission, *The Meeting of Wellington and Blücher*, appear to have seriously affected Maclise's health and precipitated his death in 1870.

Despite the impact of the Industrial Revolution and the increased efficiency of marine steam engines, sailing ships continued to be built until the turn of the century, giving added contrast to the compositions of those artists aware of the transitional nature of this period. There also developed a number of artists who could see an inherent beauty in the new steamships, especially the graceful passenger and emigrant ships. Paintings of naval vessels continued to have a universal appeal, if only because a navy, especially the British Royal Navy, represented the standing and authority of the country to which it belonged. With the increased overseas colonialism which became almost a hallmark of 19th-century European history, travel between countries invariably involved at some stage passage in a ship, and a navy was at this time the only means by which a country's investments and people could be maintained and protected. This meant that an awareness of one's navy was not restricted to specialists or those employed at sea. The navy instilled a sense of patriotic pride, and its ships continued to be popular subjects for paintings. Towards the end of the century and up to 1914, improvements in mass printing gave rise to an even greater demand for knowledge and illustrations of naval vessels, and the proportion of illustrated books, magazines and journals which dealt largely with naval matters in relation to other subjects far exceeds that of today or indeed the past 50 years or so. Besides giving young artists of ability the opportunity to make a living, mass printing also allowed their work to be seen by a wider audience, which increased the number of commissions received.

The Influence of Photography

The year 1839 saw the invention and thereafter the practical application of photography, sometimes as an art form in itself, but more usually as a means of recording. It had a major impact on painting and its significance was quickly recognized, although more in relation to landscape and portrait painting than to marine painting. The restrictions imposed by extended shutter speeds made marine photography extremely difficult, and even when photographers on the shore attempted to record ships at anchor, problems were caused by the motion of any object floating on water. As a result, many early marine photographs are out of focus in the foreground. Artists used photography as an extension to sketching from life and props used in the studio, and one wonders what would have been achieved by many notable marine artists if they had had access to photography, as did Sir Lawrence Alma-Tadema (1836–1912) or William Powell Frith (1819–1909). The expense and equipment needed in the early days made photography less of a threat to artists than it later became, especially in terms of the commissioning of young artists to produce illustrations of current events. Nevertheless, towards the end of the latter half of the century photography had made its mark in practically all walks of life, and artists used its naively assumed accuracy

AN AMERICAN TOPSAIL SCHOONER WITH A BRITISH SQUARE-RIGGER

William Joy (1803–67)

Royal Exchange Art Gallery, London

This lively watercolour painting, with subdued and carefully controlled colours, possibly shows an American slaver on the point of lowering her colours in surrender and acknowledgement of the far superior forces represented by the large British ship in the background. It is typical of Joy's work, particularly in the rendering of the sea; an approach adopted by many mid-19th-century marine artists. Intentionally or otherwise, it creates the impression of a rough sea which is at variance with the amount of sails set by the two vessels. The vessels themselves show Joy's understanding of ship construction; he lived for most of his life in the Isle of Wight and Hampshire areas, so was well able to study ships at first-hand. The British ship possibly shows a greater level of conviction. It is on the whole a successful composition and provides an interesting contrast to the Roux pictures reproduced in this book.

WHITBY HARBOUR, 1882
Atkinson Grimshaw (1836–93)
Richard Green Gallery, London
The great Victorian painter of harbours, docks and ports under moonlight is here represented by a painting of one of his favourite locations, which clearly shows the level of accomplishment he had achieved by concentrating on a single effect. Grimshaw's work is beautifully serene, while still capturing the flavour and atmosphere of the port.

as a reference source, in particular with ship portraits – a practice which continues to this day.

ATKINSON GRIMSHAW

Two artists who were directly influenced by the techniques of photography were Atkinson Grimshaw and Charles Napier Hemy. Although the former is not considered to have been a marine painter, he did contribute much to its development, especially in the relationship between the sea, ships and dock areas – man's dominant environment and its proximity to the sea. Hemy, on the other hand, was very much a marine painter in that he concentrated on seashore, coastal and fishing scenes, suggestive of nature and human harmony with it – although this is not to suggest that Grimshaw's work is indicative of conflict between nature and humanity, as the examples reproduced in this book show, but that there exists a distinct contrast between the two artists' work, each succeeding in conveying the peaceful and at times lonely environment created by both humanity and nature.

John Atkinson Grimshaw was born in Leeds in 1836, the son of a policeman, and after a brief spell in Norfolk he and his family moved back to Leeds. He was apparently discouraged from painting because of his parents' religious beliefs, and was therefore unable to undertake formal training, but presumably had to content himself with studying paintings and engravings in the local galleries. He was undoubtedly very keen to learn as much as possible, and the large number of exhibitions of contemporary work held in and around his home town gave him the opportunity to study current trends, if not actual techniques. The support he received from his wife, whom he married in 1858, further encouraged him to the

PRINCE'S DOCK, HULL, BY MOONLIGHT
Atkinson Grimshaw (1836–93)
Richard Green Gallery, London
Another example of the master's work, but this time showing a larger, more industrialized port. Because so many artists considered such scenes uninspiring, very few paintings give us an artist's understanding of the atmosphere of a busy port. We should therefore be grateful that Grimshaw found so much beauty in these often squalid, but strangely exciting places.

point that he decided in the early 1860s to become a professional painter. His work at this stage of his career was influenced by the styles and techniques of the Pre-Raphaelite movement, with its use of strong, vibrant colours and close attention to detail. A determination to succeed paid off, and in 1870 he was able to purchase a substantial house just outside Leeds. As his success increased, he purchased another house in Scarborough – which he then had to sell in order to settle a financial crisis – and later still a studio in London. He also travelled around various parts of Great Britain, often returning time after time to the same favourite location, which he would use as the basis for numerous paintings. Notable among these locations were Liverpool and Whitby. He died of cancer in 1893 at the age of 57, and soon after his death his reputation went into decline.

Grimshaw is known principally for his large number of paintings of moonlit scenes, not only of dock areas, but country settings too. His first attempt at such a scene is believed to be *Whitby Harbour by Moonlight*, executed in 1867. This painting fails to convince, not so much because it was his first attempt and therefore almost experimental in nature, but because he has used too much of the Pre-Raphaelite colour range, which gives this work an almost gaudy and cheap effect. A few years later, in about 1875, and with a more restricted palette, he produced the first of his major series of dockland night scenes, *Liverpool from Wapping*, a beautifully composed and atmospheric painting. Another notable example from this series is *Liverpool Quay by Moonlight*, painted in 1887 and now owned by the Tate Gallery in London. The composition is very similar, but with a narrower street; the whole is more compressed. Even the tracery of the masts, spars and rigging on the sailing ships tied

PILCHARDS
Charles Napier Hemy (1841–1917)
Tate Gallery, London
A brilliantly inspired, carefully observed and beautiful example of marine painting at its best. Although it depicts what was an almost everyday scene off the coast of south-west England at the time, it is a powerful image of outstanding artistic achievement, epitomizing one of man's oldest activities in gathering food for himself and his family.

CRAB POTS, FALMOUTH
Charles Napier Hemy (1841–1917)
N.R. Omell Galleries, London
The human figure at work was often central to Hemy's work.

alongside have an almost haunting quality, suggesting Grimshaw's awareness of the beauty to be found in the square-rigged sailing ship. Grimshaw has been severely criticized for producing so many similar moonlit paintings of docks, and while some do appear to have been painted according to a developed formula, in some cases even with a paucity of paint, the majority will bear close scrutiny and will remain as excellent records of the less salubrious areas of Victorian city life, comparable to the vivid written descriptions of Charles Dickens.

Grimshaw's imagination was not restricted to moonlit compositions which conformed solely to the formula described above. This is demonstrated by a beautifully serene study of a barque lying at anchor with a paddle-tug alongside; both are lying in a wide-open river, navigation lights burning brightly, showing in the background the intense yellow from the gas lights on the shoreline which subtly but realistically separate the night sky from the still waters of the river. The painting is called simply *At Anchor*, and also shows the extent to which Grimshaw had understood the limitations and application of a limited palette. For anyone who has experienced the tranquillity and appreciated the subdued colour changes which are so apparent when lying at anchor on a still night, this is an evocative painting, and for this writer it is reminiscent of the lower reaches of the river Clyde, possibly just up from Greenock, or indeed the artist's own favourite haunt, the river Mersey. It is a poignant realization that this masterpiece was painted in the last year of the artist's life.

It is only during the past 30 years or so that the works of Grimshaw have been given the recognition they deserve. The revival of his reputation has made his work available to a wider audience, not least through the excellent study of the artist's life and work by Alexander Robertson entitled simply *Atkinson Grimshaw*. It contains not only the best modern account of the artist's life and his techniques, but also the largest collection of quality reproductions to be brought together under one cover. There have also been two major exhibitions of the artist's work, the first in Leeds in 1979 and the second in London in 1990, which presented a marvellous opportunity to examine a substantial number of Grimshaw's works in one gallery. Let us hope that it is not too long before this exercise is repeated.

Charles Hemy and his Brothers

Charles Napier Hemy was born in Newcastle-upon-Tyne in 1841. He and his family emigrated to Australia in 1852, but Charles soon returned after spending about three years in the colony. After a short time as a seaman on a trading brig he decided to become a monk and entered the Dominican House in Newcastle, spending a total of three years between this monastery and one in Lyons in France. During this time he began to paint, and eventually decided to take up painting as a professional career. His formative training was under William Bell Scott at Newcastle School of Art and Baron Leys at Antwerp, both of whom were reasonably successful painters of historical scenes. As we have seen, Hemy's preference was for coastal scenes; he became well known for these, and achieved considerable success. After establishing himself in North Shields he eventually, in about 1883, moved down to Falmouth, where he kept a small yacht from which he would follow the fishing boats and other coastal craft out to sea, in order to draw them more accurately from life. Combined with his earlier seagoing experience, this enabled him to capture the realities of fishing from relatively small craft in heavy swells. He exhibited regularly at the Royal Academy from 1869, achieving a total of 78 paintings, and was elected an Associate Royal Academician in 1897 and a full RA in 1910. In addition, he was elected to the Royal Watercolour Society (RWS) and the Royal Institute of Painters in Watercolours (RI).

During Charles Hemy's lifetime there was never any doubt as to the standing of his work, and two of his paintings were bought for the Chantrey Bequest, *Pilchards* in 1897 and *London River* in 1904. He died in Falmouth in 1917.

The Chantrey Bequest is often mentioned in connection with the work of some of the more famous 19th-century marine artists. Because it was a major means of patronage to practising artists and thereby offered indirect encouragement, the artists who benefited from it were invariably figures of world stature within their respective fields. The Bequest was the result of the generosity of Sir Francis Leggatt Chantrey (1781–1841), who, with little or no formal education, became a highly successful and wealthy sculptor with a large and thriving practice. In his will he bequeathed £105,000 to the Royal Academy, the interest from which was to be used to purchase "works of Fine Art of the highest merit executed within the shores of Great Britain". At first the paintings so purchased were housed in the Victoria and Albert Museum, but along with other gifts and donations of paintings the Museum was finding it increasingly difficult to store them, let alone find the wall space on which to hang them. After the opening of the Tate Gallery in 1897, the Chantrey paintings were transferred there, to remain under the Tate's management on behalf of the nation. Unfortunately this does not mean that it is now possible to see these masterpieces of the marine artists' work, as a result of space restrictions and a declining interest in marine painting among those who manage the great national collections.

Charles Hemy had two brothers who also became marine painters, Thomas Marie Madawaska and Bernard Benedict, born in 1852 and 1855 respectively. Thomas's unusual third Christian name was that of the sailing ship by the same name which took the family out to Australia,

AMONG THE SHINGLES AT CLOVELLY
Charles Napier Hemy (1841–1917)
Laing Art Gallery, Newcastle-on-Tyne
Painted in 1864, this painting is a departure in approach from other examples of Hemy's work, in that it lacks the human emphasis. It is a beautifully composed and observed coastal beach scene, demonstrating that Hemy's abilities as a painter were not restricted to the sea as a working environment. The colour balance, tone control and detail of both the shingle and the cliff-tops are impressive. This work is included here in part to show that marine painting and illustration need not, and should not, be confined within the narrow parameters imposed by many theoretical art historians.

and on which he was born. Both brothers returned to England some years after Charles and eventually studied at Newcastle School of Art, but neither achieved the same degree of popularity and success as their elder brother, their work often lacking conviction almost to the point of appearing amateurish, although Thomas did exhibit a total of 17 paintings at infrequent intervals at the Royal Academy. The brothers appear to have remained in the Newcastle region for most of their professional lives, Thomas dying there in 1937 and Bernard in 1913.

COOKE'S COASTAL SCENES

The 19th century also saw what could be described as a revival of the Dutch influence in the painting of coastal and inshore scenes. In the 17th century the Dutch marine artists were understandably very much influenced by their environment, the flat, windswept lands blending almost imperceptibly into the sea. Many artists used the immediate foreshore as either a background against which to set the ships, or as a foreground from which to bring in a human element or to reinforce the local and coastal nature of many of the vessels. This concept was developed and extended by many of the 19th-century marine artists who saw the expansion of small natural harbours into more substantial ports as suitable and often attractive settings. In the early 20th century it was employed by those artists concerned primarily with the accurate recording of specific events at sea, especially important departures, arrivals and official functions. In some cases a landscape artist would be attracted to a particular headland or monument close to the sea, paint it and include the immediate surroundings as well.

An artist who excelled in the accurate and sympathetic

UNITS OF THE CHANNEL FLEET OFF THE LIZARD EARLY ON A SUMMER MORNING IN 1869
Charles Parsons Knight (1829–1897)
National Maritime Museum, London
A seaman who eventually studied painting formally, this oil painting is very much in the style of that great British marine painter William Lionel Wyllie, whose work is considered in the chapter on the 20th century. It records a specific, though insignificant, moment in time; its emphasis is very much on the effect of early morning light at sea and the way in which it overwhelmingly changes the apparent colour of the water, and is further reflected in any object, such as the fleet. The artist has achieved his aim effectively and with feeling.

treatment of coastal scenes was Edward William Cooke. Born in London in 1811, he was the son of George Cooke, an engraver whose professional and social contacts included the landscape painter Sir Augustus Wall Callcott and the watercolour painter John Sell Cotman. It was through his father that Edward acquired his knowledge of engraving, producing work for publication before the age of 10. These early engravings were studies of plants made for the *Encyclopaedia of Plants*. He had a close association with another of his father's friends, Clarkson Stanfield, whose work he admired and for whom he produced sketches. Besides all these direct influences, Cooke was also given tuition in the theory of perspective by Augustus Pugin and tuition by James Stark.

A classic and famous example of the drawing skill of Edward Cooke is evident in his publication *Fifty Plates of Shipping and Craft*, the first four of which were published in 1828, when Cooke was only 18. Not only did he choose the subjects, but he also did them from life and then transferred them onto copper for engraving, and his own written accounts would support the fact that he did all of this completely unaided. They were originally published in a series of 12 and have seen a number of reprints since; the most recent was published in 1970, with descriptive notes by the late Roger Finch, a schoolteacher who made a study of British local sailing craft. While it is indeed commendable that this publication again made available the engravings by Cooke, it is unfortunate that the quality of the originals could not be met, for some have lost the freshness which is so apparent in the original prints. A particularly notable aspect of these engravings is the movement and liveliness which Cooke conveys in each. Many engravings from this period and earlier tend to reflect the hard and severe nature of the medium, with

HASTINGS BEACH, 1876
Henry Moore (1831–1895)
Royal Exchange Art Gallery, London
This marine artist was very much concerned with the rendering of the sea and achieved some notable effects during a highly productive and successful career. This is a fresh and lively watercolour, with an unusual but effective composition

very little subtlety in tone or line, regardless of the fact that the technique does allow for both. The technique of engraving does not permit the beautifully soft and sensitive lines which can be produced by etching or traditional lithography and which make these two techniques much more applicable to marine subjects, but Cooke was able to control his use of engraving to an extent which gives them a rare quality. They are the 19th-century equivalents of Willem van de Velde the Elder's 17th-century grisailles, and of William Lionel Wyllie's etchings in the 20th century.

This series of engravings reflects the diversity of vessels which could be found in and around the coasts of Great Britain during the first half of the century, although the majority were drawn on the Thames. As with so many marine artists who were concerned with portraying exactly what they saw, the engravings, and indeed his painting as well, have proved to have a value beyond that of a contribution to the development of marine art, particularly for those engaged in nautical research. And it is this accuracy of observation, as with the Van de Veldes, which makes Cooke's work stand out. Cooke's understanding, for example, of the curve and set of a sail, is deep, while others of comparable ability tended to ignore the facts staring at them from their sketchbooks and used artistic licence on their more finished paintings.

It was in about 1829 that Cooke took up oil painting, and with his exceptional ability he quickly mastered this medium. In many respects, as a marine artist in oils, he far exceeded the abilities of Turner when, as a young man, he was producing his more realistic studies. His most famous painting, if only because it has been reproduced so many times, *Beaching a Pink on Scheveningen Beach* (1855), in the National Maritime Museum, is the result of his many

MIRANDA WORKING IN FROM THE WEILINGEN LIGHT SHIP IN A HEAVY WIND, OSTEND 1880
Barlow Moore (flourished 1863–1891)
Royal Exchange Art Gallery, London
This pleasing and lively study is by a little known marine artist who was at one time painter to the Royal Thames Yacht Club.

journeys to Holland, where he drew inspiration from the coast and its indigenous craft. It is one of those memorable paintings in which it is possible, if one has experienced it, to sense the strength of the wind and its effect on the sea on a shallow, wet and slow-rising beach. What adds to the intense dramatic effect is the detail on the vessel, which has been carefully observed not only in terms of what it is as an object, but also of how it would be affected by wind, sea and the viewpoint of the artist.

Cooke's interests were not restricted to the subjects of his drawings and paintings. He was also passionately interested in archaeology and natural history, and was elected a Fellow of the Royal Society in 1863. His standing as a painter was recognized by his election to the Royal Academy in 1864, following his election as an Associate in 1851. He died in Kent in 1880.

LE BRETON, MOZIN AND AIVAZOVSKY

A French artist who should be more widely acknowledged for the accuracy and draughtsmanship of his lithographs was Louis Le Breton, born at Douarnenez in 1818, who exhibited irregularly at the Paris Salon in the 1840s. His hand-tinted lithographs show a considerable understanding of the structure and design of ships and an ability to place them at any angle without fear of distortion. In this respect he was a far more highly accomplished illustrator than his contemporary English counterpart, Thomas Dutton, and in some respects more so than some of the later work of the Roux brothers. Not very much seems to be known about his life, but there is no doubt about the quality of his drawing, although from what few examples have been examined his oil-painting technique appears almost amateurish by comparison. It must be presumed that the majority of his surviving works remain in France. He died in 1866.

Another Frenchman noted for the high standard of his draughtsmanship was Charles Louis Mozin, who was born in Paris in 1806, and died in Trouville in 1862. He was very much a specialist in marine painting, with strong evidence of 18th-century traditions in his style. Of particular note are the beautifully observed and rendered sketches he made as reference to later paintings, or just to keep up practice. They show nothing more than what he was looking at, whether it was a fishing-vessel or masts waiting to be stepped, with no attempt to establish a pretentious style. As always, it is the artist's sketchbooks which give true evidence of his natural ability. Few of his paintings can be seen outside France, but a number of the large national collections hold examples of his work.

An artist who is regularly ignored in the standard dictionaries of marine artists is the Russian Ivan Aivazovsky (1817–1900), who was trained at the St Petersburg Academy of Arts and travelled widely around Europe, meeting Turner in 1842. He became an accomplished and highly regarded artist in his home country, concentrating almost equally on landscape and marine paintings with a strong, sometimes independently developed style reminiscent of the Romantic movement. His work has at times the strong impressionistic application of colour which Turner was prone to use so frequently during the latter part of his life, but Aivazovsky used it in more realistic and natural settings, without losing sight of what it was he was trying to depict. Besides this tenuous similarity in the use of bold primary colours there is little which links him with Turner; he has more in common with that great exponent of the Romantic movement, the German landscape painter Caspar David Friedrich (1774–1840). Aivazovsky obviously had a keen eye, for even in some of his more imaginative paintings the vessels are drawn accurately and in proportion.

PAINTERS OF THE SEA

The scientific and technological advances made during the 19th century had an effect on some artists which could be compared with today's environmental awareness. Rather than record how these changes were manifested at sea through improvements in naval architecture, they turned to nature itself and attempted to convey the continuous movement and beauty of sea and sky. In effect they became painters of the sea. There were not many of these pure sea painters, but those who did concentrate on this area of marine painting made a substantial contribution to the perception and understanding of the sea as rendered in painting. Indeed, although there has never been any great following of pure sea painters, many later artists have been influenced, directly or otherwise, by these 19th-century specialists, among them John Brett (1830–1902),

LIGHT BREEZE OFF DODMAN AT MEVAGISSEY, CORNWALL, 1881
Henry Moore (1831–95)
Royal Exchange Art Gallery, London
This oil sketch is one of Moore's successful attempts at rendering the sea. He has also managed to achieve the effect of space and distance, creating a composition which captures the tranquillity of being at sea, while still relatively close to the shore and without the loneliness of the open ocean. The way in which he has shown the shoreline, partly shrouded in mist, and the clouds above, indicate his awareness of the realities of nature and his ability to record it effectively on canvas. The palette range also reflects Moore's expertise in manipulating colour. Although not a highly finished painting it is, nevertheless, a classic example of the approach of the painters of sea, as opposed to those who concentrated on the vessels.

THE FISHERMAN, 1889
Henry Scott Tuke (1858–1929)
Nottingham Castle Museum and Art Gallery
Tuke was one of the outstanding marine artists from the Newlyn School, who successfully and powerfully captured the relationship between man and the sea in all weathers and in all conditions. If he had a preference, it was for recording the boating and fishing scenes which predominated in and around Falmouth where he lived and worked. The example shown here is a marvellous rendition; the fisherman, whose face is full of character, in an excellently drawn dinghy, the sailing ships lying awaiting orders in Falmouth Roads and the backdrop of Cornish hills all combine to make this pleasing and restful image.

Henry Moore (1831–95) and David James, who flourished between 1885 and 1900. The first two became very well established, while David James is little known in comparison. Others included Edwin Hayes (1819–1904) and Thomas Rose Miles, who flourished between 1869 and 1888.

John Brett was born in Surrey and joined the Royal Academy Schools as a student in 1853. His early work consisted in the main of landscapes with a strong evidence of Pre-Raphaelite influence, as in his first major work to be accepted and hung at the Royal Academy (in 1856), *The Stonebreaker*. This painting, with its meticulous attention to detail and intense realism, also shows how Brett was influenced by photography. In fact he became quite an accomplished and keen amateur photographer, besides being also very interested in science – he was elected a fellow of the Royal Astronomical Society in 1871. From about 1869 he increasingly took to the painting of marine and coastal views, in both oils and watercolour, becoming something of an expert in composing scenes with little more than the sea and sky. His ability to observe from nature was excellent, and he was also able to convey in his painting the mood and atmosphere of the British coasts. His work is variable in quality, but this may be due to the need for constant practice and experimentation necessary when attempting to paint the sea effectively. Besides his exquisite, moving and deservedly famous *Britannia's Realm*, which he painted in 1880, he was equally at home with the less romantic images of the sea. He died in London in 1902 after a successful career which included the exhibition of 114 works in the Royal Academy over a period from the age of 26 until the year before his death.

An artist often unfairly criticized for sometimes producing inferior work during his lifetime was Henry Moore,

LUGGERS PICKING UP MOORINGS, 1886
Allan J. Hook (flourished late 19th century)
Royal Exchange Art Gallery, London
Little seems to be known about this artist, but from this painting it may be assumed that he worked in the west of England and possibly Cornwall in particular; indeed, he may have been involved to a lesser extent with the artists from the Newlyn School, for there is some similarity in technique and style. It is certain that the small fishing boats depicted here are from Penzance in Cornwall; this is substantiated not only by their rig, but, more importantly, by the registration of the lugger in the foreground. It is included here for no other reason than that it is an excellent example of marine painting in the late 19th century.

born in York from a family of painters. In fact, it would not be unreasonable to call Henry Moore possibly the greatest of the 19th-century pure sea painters. Like Brett, with whom he often associated, even though their work is noticeably very different, Henry Moore had a careful eye and was able to capture the mood of the environment in his paintings. His career developed in much the same way as Brett's, in that he started his professional career as a landscape painter, working in both oils and watercolours. A particular example of his beautiful coastal scenes is *Catspaws off the Land*, in the Tate Gallery. It was painted in 1885 as a result of one of the numerous cruises he made in friends' yachts, and was purchased under the terms of the Chantrey Bequest in the same year. It is a really beautiful painting, showing an excellent use of the juxtaposition of the rocky and quickly rising shore with the calm sea of an almost windless midsummer's day, with two fishing craft drifting across the picture. In complete contrast, his diploma painting for election as a full Academician to the Royal Academy in 1893, *Summer Breeze in the Channel*, shows a short, choppy sea with two sailing ships in the distance to add to the scale and distance. The tone values in the sea are less apparent, which tends to make the form and movement more reliant on the colours, a less effective method. He died in Margate in June 1895.

Very little is known of the life of David James, which is surprising, since some sources state that he was a prolific painter. His work is outstanding and stands up well to comparison with Brett's or Moore's work, although very little of it can be seen in national collections or has been reproduced in any of the standard books on marine painting. He is particularly known for his studies taken from the immediate shoreline, and looking straight out to

THE LAST EVENING
Jacques Joseph Tissot (1836–1902)
Guildhall Art Gallery, London
This may be the first time that a Tissot painting has been included in a book on marine painting. Every study about this eminent Victorian artist has concentrated on the human element in his work and has paid little attention to the settings in which he placed them and, indeed, the context of the story his paintings told. This marvellously descriptive painting is full of carefully observed emotion and detail.

sea. Sailing ships or steam vessels are included to give scale and distance to his compositions.

In the late 18th century and throughout the 19th there developed almost a breed of artists devoted entirely to the painting of ship portraits. With the constantly increasing number of ships being built, the demand by owners and captains for accurate studies created an almost separate industry, and because it is clearly recognized as a separate development within marine painting as a whole, it will be covered by a brief separate chapter. It is only mentioned at this stage because it is important to understand that this style or technique developed concurrently with the more traditionally accepted notions of marine painting.

Generally speaking, developments in marine painting in Western Europe and outside Great Britain were slow, and lacked the British impetus. The Netherlands had long since failed to produce any notable artists, although the tradition continued with some landscape artists who occasionally undertook a marine or coastal subject. In Germany the traditions remained very much with the landscape, and the Romantic associations of an earlier age. The lack of a substantial coastline and the initial reliance on other nations' vessels made marine painting very much a local affair, and as with so many other countries the emphasis was on the ship portrait first, rather than ships and the sea as an integral whole. With one or two notable exceptions, some of whom have already been mentioned, Great Britain yet again dominated the field of marine painting.

The Newlyn School

The marine painting of the 19th century cannot be touched upon without a brief introduction to the Newlyn School of artists, even though the school is often ignored in the majority of standard reference sources. While in some respects this school bridges the 19th and 20th centuries, it was established in the former, and the professional reputation of many of its followers had also been established long before the school as such came into being. The artist who will always be associated with the Newlyn School is Stanhope Forbes, who was born in Dublin in 1857. He was trained at Dulwich School and at the Lambeth School of Art, before joining the Royal Academy Schools in 1876. Forbes was not in any way a marine artist, but concerned himself very much with everyday events and the people who made them happen.

Much of the style and technique which became synonymous with this school developed from the influence and commitment to French *plein air* painting – painting in the open air rather than within the confines of a studio – after Forbes' extended visits to northern France. The landscape and atmosphere of Brittany had a great attraction for Forbes, and it was the similarity to Brittany which eventually decided him to settle in Cornwall in general

A STRONG BREEZE IN THE CHANNEL
Thomas Jacques Somerscales (1842–1927)
Harris Museum and Art Gallery (?)
The square-rigged sailing ship in her natural environment and depicted by a marine artist who excelled in combining two elements: a man-made object with nature. And Somerscales achieved this with consummate skill and natural ability. The sense of balance in his compositions, the tonal values, the movement and depth of his seas, and the conviction of reality of his ships, all combine to make the vast majority of his work into inspiring and moving examples of the marine artist's skill.

and Newlyn in particular. Of course, the more favourable climate, compared to that of London or other regions of England, suited painting outdoors. A development from France which Forbes and others took to Cornwall was the use of the square-brush technique, which has become more recognizable as being from Cornwall than from its actual place of origin. The technique created soft-edged paintings with much atmosphere. Forbes' greatest achievement and also the one important painting which warrants his inclusion in this book, is his *A Fish Sale on a Cornish Beach*, in the Plymouth City Museum and Art Gallery, which he began in February 1885 and painted primarily *on the beach*, in defiance of all that nature could throw at him. It was received with tremendous applause at the Royal Academy in the same year, and it was this painting which led to the recognition of the artists working in Newlyn and established Forbes as the leader. This painting was at first considered suitable for purchase through the Chantrey Bequest, but the trustees eventually decided against it because of its strong foreign influences. This was the view taken by some in the British art establishment at the time of the Newlyn School, even though nothing could have been further from the truth. It is an example of how the parameters of marine painting can and should be extended to include those aspects of life associated indirectly with the sea. Besides this large work, Forbes produced a number of other paintings with a nautical feel or setting to them, many of them based on what was then the ever-present fleet of inshore sailing trawlers and drifters.

The close proximity of Newlyn to the sea and the town's reliance on the fishing industry, as well as the nearby ports and harbours, gave at the time an unrivalled opportunity for artists seeking variable subjects which

ENTERING INTO THE BAY OF VALPARAISO
Thomas Jacques Somerscales (1842–1927)
N.R. Omell Galleries, London
Undoubtedly the practical experience of being at sea helped Somerscales' understanding, but after studying his work there can be no question that his natural ability to convey the atmosphere and impact of a sailing ship at sea was inherent within him. In the example above, he has chosen to place the barque at a difficult angle – not only the set of her sails, but also the heel of her hull. The position of the barque, combined with the angle at which she has been drawn, directs the eye to take in the complete composition.

combined a strong human presence, and also allowed them to indulge their interest in the atmosphere of a composition. One of those from the school who has become recognized for many of his marine paintings was Henry Scott Tuke (1858–1929). He was born in York and moved to Falmouth in 1885 after training at the Slade School of Art and in Paris and Italy. He specialized in portraits and boating scenes from in and around the protected natural harbour of Falmouth. Like those of his fellow-artists from the Newlyn School, his colour application and tone control are exemplary, no doubt the result of working primarily in near-perfect light conditions. The painting he submitted to the Royal Academy in 1889, *All Hands to the Pumps*, demonstrates his natural ability to draw the human form and to compose a painting of a tense and frightening moment at sea with just the right emphasis. Rightly judged to be in keeping with the terms of the Chantrey Bequest, it was duly purchased for the nation and now resides in the Tate Gallery.

The 19th century undoubtedly produced some of the best marine painters of the western world, with artists from Great Britain dominating throughout the period, and in a comparatively short volume it is impossible to draw attention to all but a few of those who so successfully contributed to the development of this art form. There are one or two outstanding books available which cover this important period in more detail, which are listed in the Bibliography, and it is recommended that these be studied in addition to this book, which contains a high proportion of paintings which have not been reproduced before. They add further weight to the plea for marine painting to be given the same extended treatment and exposure as other subject areas within the history of art, especially in the 19th and early 20th centuries.

OFF VALPARAISO
Thomas Jacques Somerscales (1842–1927)
Tate Gallery, London
Arguably one of the finest marine paintings of the 19th century. The whole concept of this painting is near perfect. It effectively and overwhelmingly epitomizes man's most beautiful of creations in its natural setting. Somerscales painted it in 1899 and it was bought for the Chantrey Bequest in the same year. Sadly it has not been displayed for a number of years.

HMS *ARETHUSA*, 1849
William Frederick Mitchell (1845–1914)
Royal Exchange Art Gallery, London
Mitchell could be described as an English Roux, but although his work is of a high standard in terms of both accuracy and the application of watercolour, it somehow lacks the freshness and movement apparent in the work of the French family. Much of his work was the result of commissions from serving naval officers. Historically it is very important, for it offers valuable information about the appearance of naval warships.

NORTH AMERICAN DEVELOPMENTS

The original and early immigrants from predominantly West European countries settled at first on the shores of the eastern seaboard of North America, and although they brought with them many of the traditions and values associated with the Old World, the concept and foundation of an indigenous art form was a long time in coming. It would appear that for artists of even average ability, Europe remained a vast and expanding market where it continued to be possible to make a reasonably successful living. There was no need for the majority of artists to consider emigration in order to improve their prospects, and indeed there was little change for some considerable time until well into the 19th century: the focus of all major events, schools of thought and movements concerned with the arts in general remained firmly established in Europe, and in fact this continued to be the case until the outbreak of the First World War in 1914. Nevertheless, as will be seen, many talented and highly skilled marine artists did cross the Atlantic and continued their successful careers in America, but they of course had already acquired their training and had perfected their technique before emigrating.

The development of marine painting in particular in America during the 18th century was almost non-existent; the main bulk of painting was devoted to the execution of portraits of the growing number of wealthy merchants, as had been the case during the preceding century, although on a smaller scale. Internal trade expansion was for a long time dependent on continued links with Europe, especially England, and thus the majority of the merchant class had connections with shipping, either through ownership,

HMS *BELLEROPHON* , 1818
William Frederick Mitchell (1845–1914)
Royal Exchange Art Gallery, London
Another example of the ship-portrait style adopted by this prolific painter. Close examination will reveal Mitchell's tendency to paint quite freely in the detail of his hulls, and yet he was meticulous in the way he painted the gradated washes on the sails and the care and accuracy he applied when depicting the rigging. His skies are classic examples of overlaid and gradated washes of transparent colour.

shipbuilding or both. This connection was often evident from the use of a marine-style backdrop to set off the portrait proper. In many cases these portraits were as accomplished as any being painted in Europe at the time, but clearly the artists concerned had little time or interest in things nautical, for the ships shown are often extremely crude, even allowing for the fact that they constitute an insignificant part of the painting. Nevertheless, it has been shown that through these paintings marine painting eventually came to be seen as a separate art form in North America.

The next stage of development was the contribution made by a desire to record the events of the American Revolution in 1776, as well as those which preceded and followed it. The recording of history through painting was firmly established in Europe, and it is no surprise that the profound and significant events taking place in a vast new country gaining its independence should be portrayed by its artists. However, the lack of formal training for artists, unless they had the means to travel to Europe, meant that many were self-taught or acquired part of their skills through working as ship- or house-painters. Those who were fortunate enough to be trained in Europe, or at least have contact with European artists, did achieve a comparable standard. However, for those who remained in America it is noticeable that the level of sophistication in the manipulation of paint, whether oil or watercolour, was extremely low, as indeed was the draughtsmanship on many occasions. Examples at the turn of the 19th century also appear to show a poor level of understanding of tone values and colour balance, although it could be argued that in the latter case this was intentional.

SAILING SHIPS ON THE ATLANTIC
Patrick von Kalckreuth (flourished 1890 to early 20th century)
Christie's, London.

CAREENING AT LOW TIDE
G.R. Evans (*c.* 1900)
Christie's, London.

A FRIGATE OFF LIVERPOOL
Robert Salmon (1775–c.1845)
National Maritime Museum, London

Salmon was a well-known ship-portrait painter who worked on both sides of the Atlantic producing oil paintings of ships, often in a harbour mouth or in an estuary. Salmon's work varies in quality, although there is always a common style distinctive throughout. This particular example, possibly showing a French-designed ship under the British flag, has a more stylized sea and preponderance of a yellow hue to the whole image. The ship is accurately and carefully drawn and rendered, as are the surrounding craft and town. However, the complete painting appears cramped and almost excessively busy, even though the immediate activity is limited. This practice of filling the canvas with as much of the vessel as possible is typical of the vast majority of ship-portrait painters, but the degree of success with which it works as a painting depends very much on the way the ship is used in relation to the setting in which the artist places it. Although there is a certain naïve charm about it, this painting of Salmon's does not work as well as many of his others.

ROBERT SALMON

A notable marine painter who bridged the American–English quality divide was Robert Salmon, born in Whitehaven, Cumberland, in 1775, who first came to notice in 1806 in Liverpool (although a marine painter by the same name exhibited at the Royal Academy in 1802). His earlier life is unrecorded; it has been suggested that he spent his formative years in his father's jeweller's shop or possibly at sea, although no evidence exists to confirm either. After Liverpool, Salmon moved around England quite extensively before eventually emigrating to America in 1828. He arrived in Boston on 1 January 1829, and remained until 1840, by which time he had built up a successful practice in a studio overlooking the harbour; he concentrated primarily on ship portraits in named rather than in imaginary locations. He also painted topographical views based very much on his time at Liverpool, Greenock and Boston; these locations also provided the backdrop to many of his ship portraits. Because of failing eyesight he returned to Europe, where he died some time between 1845 and 1848.

Salmon's work is very precise and shows meticulous attention to detail, without in any way detracting from the composition, and as such are excellent examples of early 19th-century marine paintings. His draughtsmanship shows that he had more than a superficial interest in his subjects; the hulls are beautifully observed and the set of the sails and rigging are all accurately recorded. There is no doubt that he knew the principles of handling a ship under sail. Because of Salmon's close attention to detail, many of his ship portraits are excellent reference sources for establishing the appearance and design of particular ships; this, considering the dearth of reliable information on merchant sailing ships for this period, gives his works a historical importance equal to their value as marine paintings. Considered as an artist, Salmon was not just a recorder of ship portraits, but used his understanding and appreciation of light and shade to produce beautifully convincing effects. His work is also noted for the human element; all his vessels are shown with seamen about their daily business, and often with other nautical activities going on as well. His work, while founded in the English and Scottish Schools of the 17th and 18th centuries, clearly shows the progressive influence of the Dutch (obviously including the Van de Veldes) as well as of Canaletto, especially in the rendering of water within the confines of harbours or deep-water estuaries and in the detail applied to the architecture of the harbours he so often used as a backdrop.

Robert Salmon's attention to detail was not confined to his paintings, for he kept a catalogue of the works he produced between 1806 and 1840; the entries varying in detail. During this period he painted at least 999 canvases – an output which, indirectly, contributed much to the development of marine painting in America.

COMMODORE DANCE DISCOVERING THE FRENCH FLEET UNDER REAR-ADMIRAL COMTE DE LINOIS, 5 FEBRUARY, 1804
Thomas Buttersworth (1768–1842)
Christie's, London

Although Buttersworth understood the ships he painted, he has never been considered in the top ranks of marine artists. His work is included here not only because it covers the transitional period from the 18th to the 19th centuries, but it also allows comparative study with other paintings reproduced in this book, so that the reader may more fully appreciate the diversity of skills and talent in the broad spectrum of marine painting and illustration. Incidentally, at first glance it would appear that you are looking at only two ships repeating themselves, rather than the twelve which actually exist.

THE HUDSON RIVER SCHOOL

The Romantic Movement was late arriving in America, and continued longer, not surprisingly considering the historical factors and their profound consequences. But when the concepts of the Movement did eventually filter through to artists, some took them on with an intensity rarely seen in Europe. An example is offered in the work by Thomas Cole, *The Voyage of Life: Childhood, Youth, Manhood and Old Age*, painted in 1842, and now in the National Gallery of Art in Washington, DC. These four paintings are very much on the periphery of marine painting, but are mentioned here because they demonstrate the crude use of too extensive a palette, even though it is obvious that Cole had some drawing ability. Other examples of Cole's work include coastal and river scenes but with the emphasis always on the shore, be it in the foreground or background. Cole himself was not a native of the country in which he chose to live and work, but came from Bolton in England, where he was born in 1801. He emigrated to Philadelphia before finally settling in New York, where he died in 1848, although he had returned to Europe at least once. He is noted in America for his leadership of the Hudson River School, a name which was more to do with the location than with a particular style, technique or concept. The name was given to a group of artists who were not all necessarily well-known or important, and who congregated on the area of the Hudson River Valley, some way from the sea, where they devoted their efforts to painting the surrounding groves and riversides. It was partly an attempt to develop a greater affinity with nature and record it with visual accuracy.

The second generation of the Hudson River School manifested a combination of the influences of the first generation and the importance which was being attached to the coast and shoreline as a stimulus for painting. An artist of some distinction from this period was John Frederick Kensett, who was born in New Hampshire in 1818 and, like Cole before him, concentrated on river and coastal scenes, although never to the same standards as those practising their art on the same subjects in England. He and his work had a great deal of influence on the development of the American school of marine painting, which began to be established and identified during the early part of the second half of the 19th century. Kensett himself was not restricted in his own personal development by the comparative limitations of his country, for he travelled extensively in Europe, remaining principally in England and Rome for seven years. This stay greatly influenced his style and technique, for there is a definite improvement in his work after he returned to America in 1847, although he continued in the excessive use of colour, almost a tradition with the Hudson River School. Much of his later work is almost photographic in its outline and detail, but there is no evidence that he used photography as a reference source in any way. The application of colour appears to be through glazes built up to achieve the required density, for much of his work reveals a tendency even to exceed reality – almost presaging the American artists of the first half of the 20th century who developed the glazing technique to unprecedented levels. He was elected a member of the National Academy in 1849 and died in New York in 1872.

Another artist from the same generation as Kensett, and one who developed into a more obvious marine artist, albeit still concentrating on the shoreline, was Frederic Edwin Church, born in Connecticut in 1826. He was a pupil of Thomas Cole, through whom he acquired a grounding in the execution of technique and style, but he was soon progressing beyond the dull and limiting imagination of his teacher. He also travelled to Europe and was much impressed by the work of Turner; some sources suggest his work was inspired by Turner, but there is little evidence to support this theory. He was fond of sunsets and sunrises, but lacked the skill and appreciation of colour which Turner used so dramatically in his later works. Church's paintings remain committed to detail and reality, and if it were not for the colour imbalance, his paintings would have had an even greater quality about them. However, his colour balance was not always impaired or amateurish, and he was able to capture accurately that almost unattainable glow which is so noticeable when observing sunrises and sunsets from nature. If it had been invented at the time, one would be tempted to suggest that he used colour photography as a primary reference source, because the realistic effect of the skies in some of his paintings is almost uncanny.

Marine painting in America during the 19th century cannot be discussed without reference to Fitz Hugh Lane, who is considered to be the first native-born marine painter of any substance. He was also of the second generation of the Hudson River School, born in Cape Ann, Massachusetts, in 1804; his ancestors had settled in Gloucester in 1623. Lane's work has been compared in favourable terms with that of Robert Salmon, even to the point of suggesting a line of influence. This must be disputed if only from the point of accuracy in the proportions of Lane's square-rigged vessels, which so often show somewhat stunted rigs and excessive beams. Fundamental inaccuracies are often overlooked by art historians because of gaps in their own knowledge and understanding, but when making a true assessment of a marine painter, such faults cannot be ignored, no matter how great the painter's technical excellence. Nevertheless, the detail with which Lane's ships are rigged does suggest that his knowledge of shipping and possibly naval architecture in general was reasonably advanced.

Be this as it may, Fitz Hugh Lane was a very successful artist during his own lifetime; his work fell into disfavour after his death in 1865, but this was the case with many early 19th-century artists and does not imply any criticism of Lane in particular. He is now appreciated by many, both

BOSTON
John W. Hill (flourished early 19th century); engraved by
C. Mottram
Christies, London.

THE FOUR-MASTED SCHOONER *"SENATOR SULLIVAN"*
William Pierce Stubbs (1842–1909)
Penobscot Marine Museum, Maine

THE AMERICAN BARQUE *MENDOTA*
Louis Roux (1817–1903)
Penobscot Marine Museum. Maine
There is no connection between this Roux and the family of marine artists by the same name. His style is similar, but although his accuracy is comparable, his work appears stiffer.

for the quality of his work and, perhaps more importantly, for his status in the foundation and development of a distinctive North American style of marine painting. Lane received limited tuition in painting, although he no doubt acquired some guidance through his association with other young artists in the Boston area.

Lane did not limit himself to painting in one particular medium, but experimented, and was successful in a number of media, including oils, watercolours, lithographs and pencil studies. His subject-matter was equally diverse, and extended beyond pure or traditional marine paintings or ship portraits. Among his works can be found naval engagements, landscapes, portraits, business cards and book illustrations. Lane was able to draw and print his own lithographs, thanks to his apprenticeship with an important firm of lithographers in Boston, and this ability enhanced both his standing and success. American sources often consider Lane's best work to have been completed during the last 10 years of his life, and to a certain extent this is true, but it does depend very much on what criteria are used. When compared with marine painting in Europe during the same period, Lane's work is distinctive with its almost independently developed style, but still lacks conviction and impact, which is again typical of the much slower progress of the genre.

European Influences

Chapters Four and Five gave an introduction to the important Roux family of watercolour painters, who concentrated on realistic ship portraits. A vast majority of the commissions this family received were from American masters and crew members of vessels trading to or calling at Marseilles. The family were not alone in this occupation, and others who achieved the same degree of expertise are now recognized as of equal importance. Many of these watercolour studies crossed the Atlantic and were seen by American artists, who not only admired the style, but endeavoured to emulate it. The influence of the Mediterranean artists was therefore soon evident in the work of a number of American artists, especially during the early part of the century, but few reached the same level of general draughtsmanship or understanding of wave movement. The reason could be that there were few opportunities for

THE AMERICAN SHIP *AMERICA*, 1804
Ange-Joseph Antoine Roux (1765–1835)
Peabody Museum of Salem
Although not as colourful as the watercolour opposite, this exquisite study of the ship at anchor is excellent and is highly representative of Ange-Joseph's vast output.

young artists to train or become apprenticed, and thereby acquire the necessary guidance in order to progress.

In addition to the influences and traditions of the French, including the French Romantic Movement, Dutch influences are said to have filtered through into the work of some American marine artists, in particular through those artists who emigrated from Europe. Successful and less successful artists practising the genre in Europe could not but be influenced in turn by those whose development could be traced back to the Dutch of the 17th century. Charles Brooking and Nicholas Pocock are two who come readily to mind.

Two notable marine artists whose work clearly demonstrates the Dutch line of influence, and whose style was decidedly European, were Thomas Birch and Thomas Thompson. Both men were born in England in 1799; Birch emigrated with his father from his home city of London when he was 15. No record of Thompson's arrival in America has been found. Birch had the distinct advantage of having a father who was an engraver and miniaturist, from whom he acquired his basic knowledge; he helped his father with a series of engraved views in and around Philadelphia. By his early 20s Birch had set himself up in his own studio, concentrating initially on portraits, but soon expanding into landscapes and the occasional seascape or naval engagement, especially during the war of 1812. Without any knowledge of the sea or ships, and living some distance from the sea, Birch found it necessary to research his marine paintings, and the relative positions of the ships may be reasonably accurate, although the majority of his paintings show a poor understanding of the drawing of ships. His palette lacks the control and finesse of Brooking or Pocock, and his seas are not those of a specialist marine artist. Birch was, nevertheless, a successful and popular painter in his adopted country. He died in America in 1851.

Thomas Thompson was a more accomplished draughtsman than his contemporary, and although records indicate that he was very much a specialist marine artist, few of his works have survived. Those which are known to us again show a tendency to concentrate on coastal scenes and ports. One in particular, *Scene from the Battery with a Portrait of the Frigate* "Franklin", *74 guns*, executed in *c.*1838 (Metropolitan Museum of Art, New York), shows Thompson's more advanced knowledge and understanding of ship design. His ships have solidity and conviction, but the comparatively narrow channel and, more importantly, the wind conditions which Thompson has depicted convey more dramatic effect than reality, for all the ships, whether square-rigged or fore-and-aft, have far too much canvas set. Seamanship under sail in such conditions would not be the most enjoyable or relaxing of occupations. The composition is not as carefully controlled as one would like, for the eye tends to wander, seeking out a fixed focal point which does not exist. Thompson died in 1852.

JAMES BUTTERSWORTH

A comparatively little-known Anglo-American marine artist whose work has achieved greater recognition in his adopted country than in his country of birth is James Edward Buttersworth, the son of the English sailor-artist Thomas Buttersworth (1768–1842). J. E. Buttersworth was born in 1817, probably in London, and was undoubtedly taught by his father, for there is great similarity in style, especially in the younger painter's earlier works. Once married and with a growing family, Buttersworth moved around London and the outlying districts before deciding to emigrate to America some time between 1845 and 1847. He settled in West Hoboken, New York, where he died in 1894.

Buttersworth's work varies considerably both in artistic quality and in accuracy. At times his work is almost "primitive" and appears to be that of someone who was predominantly self-taught and without any major artistic influences; at others its freshness and spontaneity suggest a deep empathy and understanding with the chosen subject. His ship portraits, especially of square-riggers and naval vessels, lack the crispness of detail and artistic beauty of Robert Salmon's work. So often they are dull, toneless studies which look stiff and without feeling, reminiscent of many dark, oppressive 19th-century boardrooms. His seas too show little evidence of the developments which had taken place in England, and almost seem to date from an earlier time. A very distinctive feature of practically all Buttersworth's work is the way in which he depicted sails, showing them as immaculately curved and uncreased pieces of canvas, all conforming to a uniform pattern, with an evenly gradated tone to accentuate the curve. No cast shadows are used, regardless of the conditions apparent in the sky, and the tone values used on the sails of vessels shown during stormy weather or poor light conditions remain the same, in complete contrast to reality.

However, a number of pencil sketches, highlighted with white body-colour, have survived which show a totally different approach. These sketches, completed in 1851, are part of a series of 17, now at The Dauntless Club in Essex, Connecticut. They show a number of different fore-and-aft rigged yachts, a topsail schooner and a barque-rigged yacht. Not only are they beautifully rendered and observed, but they are also full of life and movement – some even include cast shadows and other closely observed effects of light and shade. Why Buttersworth was not able – or willing – to develop and explore the underlying technique of these pencil drawings and transfer it to his finished oil paintings must remain a mystery. There is some limited evidence which shows that the natural drawing ability apparent in the sketches was used in paintings; a good example is one entitled *American Ship-of-the-Line off Belem Castle, Leaving Boston*, which Buttersworth painted in about 1860. Interestingly, it is a small oil painting on millboard, but it shows a three-decker from the starboard bow sailing on the port tack, with the light source coming from right-to-left across the painting. Three other vessels are also shown: a small three-masted ship, heeling severely in the freshening breeze, and, unusually, two luggers. While no cast shadows have been included on the sails of the principal ship, there are strong contrasting shadows and tones on the sea and to the hulls of the vessels. While slightly crude in its rendering, the sea does at least add to the impression of a freshening breeze and conforms to the general wind direction. Overall, this painting complements the sketches and lacks the flat and repetitive nature of much of Buttersworth's work.

WINSLOW HOMER

Every so often an artist comes along whose work captures the imagination of a public not usually interested in painting, and whose reputation continues to grow long after his death. Such an artist was Winslow Homer, whose work is possibly more recognizable and identifiable than his name, so often and so widely reproduced are his works today, on both sides of the Atlantic. He represents the height of American 19th-century marine painting. He was born in Boston in 1836 and died in Prout's Neck, Maine, in 1910, and between those years he built an exceptional reputation. His early ability to draw was put to good use during his training in a lithographer's shop, where he also became very adept at using tone values effectively.

Homer travelled to Europe in 1866, a journey which

AN AMERICAN PACKET BOAT ▷
James Edward Buttersworth (1817–1894)
Christie's, London
A typical example of the approach of this popular marine artist. Very much in the style of the 18th-century, it lacks the sophistication of much of the century being covered in this chapter.

FISHERFOLK ON THE BEACH AT CULLERCOATS, TYNEMOUTH, 1881
Winslow Homer (1836–1910)
Addison Gallery of American Art, Massachusetts
One of the great American figures in painting, Homer is not considered a specialist marine artist because of the wide variety of his other work. However, his marines compare favourably with those of his peers who did specialize. This example shows the freshness and spontaneity he was able to bring to his work when working from life, in this case during a visit to the north-east coast of England during the latter part of his life.

further extended his understanding of drawing and painting; he was receptive to any influences which might improve his own technique and style, and in fact his greatest influence came from Japanese prints rather than any European developments. Before his European tour Homer was employed during the American Civil War as a war artist, although his drawings from this traumatic period of America's history concentrated on the soldiers' life at camp rather than military actions. He did not, however, see the war through, but increasingly concerned himself with his own development, which eventually led to his visit to Europe and France in particular. Besides being accomplished as an engraver and lithographer, Homer also handled watercolours and oils with equal dexterity.

During his earlier years as a professional artist he supplemented his income from paintings by working for magazines, and this seems to have influenced his compositions in later life, which in turn have influenced generations of American illustrators since. Some of his more notable pieces would not appear out of date if reproduced alongside late 20th-century illustrations. Although Homer did not restrict his output to marine subjects, those he did paint were more often than not images of the relationship between humans and small craft and the sea; the craft themselves ranged from small working boats to the less pretentious yachts. He also touched upon coastal and river scenes, and the wildlife associated with the sea, in some cases as a result of extended visits to Canada. He also travelled to England in 1881, spending two years in Tynemouth, a small fishing village on the north-east coast.

Much of Homer's work can be seen as a progression towards his most famous painting, *The Gulf Stream*, which he executed in 1899 and which epitomizes his style and technique, even though he continued to paint for a further

THE GREAT WHITE FLEET, 1892
Frederick Schiller Cozzens (1856–1928)
Courtesy of Frank Oppel
Cozzens is better known in America for his yachting scenes, and this example of his work demonstrates his wider subject range within marine painting. It is worth comparing this with the work by William Mitchell reproduced here; overall it lacks Mitchell's stiffness, and is more of an attempt to consider the composition as an image, rather than a ship portrait in a semblance of a natural setting.

decade. The painting is very dramatic and represents the final work in an unplanned series which attempts to convey not just an image but also a statement by the artist.

The distinguished American art historian John Wilmerding has remarked: "In the 17th century power of the sea belonged largely to the Dutch; in the 18th it passed to the English; and in the 19th to the Americans." He goes on to conclude that there is a direct relationship between sea power and the epoch of marine painting in each country. This is in my view an extraordinary over-simplification of naval history, especially in relation to the Dutch. As far as the Americans were concerned, they were not to achieve the status of a major world sea power until almost the end of the century, and if there is some corresponding link between the two, then it must be understood that the genre of marine painting did not achieve anything like the same degree of perfection as could be found in Europe, especially in England, which was in reality the dominant sea power in the world until the early years of the Second World War. In reality it was not until the second quarter of the 20th century that American marine artists were found to be producing carefully observed and rendered paintings on a large scale. Today we have a "North American School of Historical Marine Painting" which, overall, has no equal.

CHAPTER SIX

The Naïve and Ship-Portrait Painters 1800–1940

THE CONCEPT OF THE TERMS "NAÏVE" AND "PRIMITIVE" IS OFTEN open to confusion as a result of the differing interpretations placed on their meaning by art historians. In the context of this present study, "naïve" is used to describe those artists whose style and technique developed independently of any formal training, and who did not necessarily come under the influences of either separate schools or artists who had already reached a maturity of style, other than possibly contact with their own kind. Naïve painters are often referred to as "amateurs". As has been recognized so far, the concept of influence, training and maturity of style is not relevant to an artist's standing as a "professional" or "amateur", whatever might be the heading or group with which the artist in question may now be associated.

NAÏVE MARINE PAINTERS

However, the contribution made by naïve painters of the sea to man's wider understanding and interpretation of the sea and ships is very limited, as is their contribution to our historical knowledge. One reason is a general lack of drawing ability, regardless of their knowledge of the subjects they painted. In fact many of the paintings represented by this group show only a limited advance in the understanding of perspective and the interpretation of three-dimensional information on a two-dimensional surface from that of the Egyptians of 2000 BC. Nevertheless, some naïve works offer a certain decorative pleasure, and there is in many an almost childlike quality which heightens their appeal beyond that of marine painting as a specialist genre.

It is extremely difficult to define characteristics which predominate in the work of the naïve artists of the sea, other than the comparative crudity with which ships are drawn – usually as flat, orthographic, but inaccurate, elevations. If the vessel is a sailing ship, its masts and sails are drawn in an equally mechanistic manner. Indeed, some examples show evidence of the use of drawing instruments, although this is not to suggest that their use should be condemned, or that only naïve artists used them. Drawing aids are often considered anathema and artists criticized when they are used today, yet many of the great masters of the past used them when they considered them helpful. Other common factors are a lack of contrast, depth and colour balance. The colour itself is often applied flat, primary and secondary colours used within clearly defined outlines.

Because many naïve artists were seamen and others without formal education and training, many of the works which are now housed in national collections around the world are unsigned and will forever remain anonymous. But, such works did not always go unrecognized as contributing to man's understanding and development of art *per se*, apart from their limited value to marine painting. Much of this initial recognition was due to the wealthy classes of an earlier time looking patronizingly at the attempts of socially "inferior" classes at so-called intellectual activities and finding the results "charming" – a common enough occurrence in the late 19th and early 20th centuries. William Gaunt identifies a retired French toll-station inspector from outside Paris, Henri Rousseau (*Le Douanier*, 1844–1910), as being one of the first to receive recognition for the quality of his painting, although he did not restrict himself purely to marine studies. Many of his works have found their way into the Louvre in Paris, even though they are more akin to what might be objectively described as advanced children's paintings.

As mentioned in Chapter Five, many 19th-century American artists are considered naïve or primitive, and many of these spare-time and professional artists lacked the means to travel to Europe, working very much in isolation and primarily for family and friends. They received little if any recognition during their lifetime, although many now constitute part of important national collections. An example of one of these naïve artists was James Bard, born in New York in 1815, whose work can be found in the National Gallery of Art, Washington, DC, the Peabody Museum of Salem and the Mariners Museum at Newport News. Bard was obsessed with the steamships which he was able to observe from his home overlooking the Hudson River, and it has been said that during his artistic career he made a

THE GERMAN THREE-MASTED BARQUE *CERES* SAILING IN A CHOPPY SEA

Antonio Nicolo Gasparo Jacobsen (1850–1921)

N.R. Omell Galleries, London

A good example of the hard, sharp approach adopted and developed by this successful and prolific ship-portrait painter working from New York, and with examples in many national collections around the western world. The rendering of the sea is particularly typical of Jacobsen's technique and he used it on the vast majority of his paintings, regardless of the sails set on the ships and the implied wind conditions! However, this style, especially in relation to the ship, is useful historically because it affords an opportunity to determine with reasonable accuracy the appearance and design of the ship. While the rigging and sails may be accurate technically, the latter are stiff and without movement almost to the point of appearing to be made of some totally inflexible material. Yet there is a certain charm and appeal in this painting, which is reflected in the constant demand for paintings in this style, typical as it is of ship-portrait painters.

record of practically every steamer which used the port. The quality of finish and detail in both his ships and settings vary considerably, from an extreme primitive approach to a more sophisticated descriptive style.

In England a naïve painter whose work has achieved some status by its inclusion in the Tate Gallery, London, the National Maritime Museum, Greenwich, and Auckland City Art Gallery, is that of Alfred Wallis. He was born in Devonport in 1855 and at the age of nine went to sea in an Atlantic steamer as a cabin-boy. He then became a fisherman on luggers working out of the small harbours on the Cornish coast, and finally a marine store dealer in St Ives. Basically an illiterate, he turned to marine painting in the late 1920s after the death of his wife, possibly to relieve the loneliness he suffered. As a naïve and very poor artist, he epitomizes the approach adopted by many, for he was able and willing to draw and paint on anything which came to hand, and not necessarily with artists' colours either, for some of his works were rendered in ships' paints. He died almost destitute in a workhouse in 1942, and, ironically when one considers how artists of all abilities are treated by society, his works are now considered extremely collectable, and are therefore very expensive, thanks to the cult which has grown around him as a modern artist. When compared to that of the American James Bard, Wallis's work is even more primitive and crude – it is merely the work of a complete amateur of limited skill, who used painting in an almost self-therapeutic manner to occupy his time, and not out of vanity, or for gain or recognition.

Ship Portraits and Their Painters

There is a distinct and notable contrast between the naïve artists described above and those who specialized in the painting of ship portraits, but the link between them in this chapter is the fact that both groups are of artists who often had no formal training. Their work also lacks cohesive reality and conviction when compared with the forceful visual statements made by the great exponents of marine painting described elsewhere in this book. However, considered as illustrators the ship-portrait painters fulfil the criteria completely, for they were concerned principally with the image and appearance of the ship rather than with her direct and unavoidable involvement with her environment. This took second place. But regardless of this, many were successful and achieved a not unreasonable living from the sale of their works on a very professional basis, even though their clientele was from a relatively small, but important and clearly defined group within society.

Within the heading of ship-portrait painters, or pierhead painters as they are sometimes referred, two separate categories can be distinguished: those whose techniques were severely restricted by their lack of drawing ability, and those who had an advanced knowledge of the application

THE BARQUE *LADY CHARLOTTE* OFF THE SOUTH STACK
Samuel Walters (1811–82)
N.R. Omell Galleries, London

Walters was not just a ship-portrait painter, but achieved some success in painting general coastal scenes as well. This example is typical of his style during his earlier years, and shows the method adopted to render the sails, which is very much in the form of rigid geometrical shapes. During the latter part of his career he drew the sails in a far less stylized manner, and many of these works compare favourably with those of the best of the ship-portrait painters.

THE BARQUE *WILLIAM PEILE*
Joseph Heard (1799–1859)
N.R. Omell Galleries, London

and techniques of their chosen medium. It must not be forgotten that there are many other artists from throughout the periods covered by this book whose work lacks the advanced application of technique combined with powers of observation in drawing and a deep understanding and awareness of the environment they attempted to visualize. However, historically they are never categorized as naïve or amateur. It is important to remember this when interpreting the work of the ship-portrait painters, for they are no less deserving of recognition and a rightful place in the history of marine painting. Indeed, it must be emphasized again that, as with so many aspects of the history and development of marine painting, there will always be an overlap and link between the styles and techniques of some individual artists, as well as an overlap between schools from different countries and periods.

Of particular importance to historians concerned with the technological development of ship design is the fact that much of the work by ship-portrait painters can be used as a contributing reference source. Obviously much would depend on the skill and accuracy of the artist, but there is no doubt that many offer far more information than those paintings which aim for an atmospheric approach. Most of these paintings were executed for people and companies associated with the sea and shipping, and who therefore expected, if not demanded, accuracy in preference to any intrinsic emotional values. Indeed, there are many instances where historians have relied solely on the details contained within a ship-portrait painting to confirm deck layouts, peculiarities of rigs and, of course, colour schemes. A good example of this is the work of J. Hord, about whom little is known other than that he flourished during the 1860s and 1870s. The detail in his paintings is keenly observed and shows a thorough understanding of ship design, but of greater relevance here is the information which can be extracted by close and careful examination.

Another whose work often includes fine detail is Marie-Edouard Adam, born in Brie-Comte-Robert, near Paris, in 1847, who worked in Le Havre as a very successful ship-portrait painter until his death in 1929. He was made an official artist to the Département de la Marine in 1886 and contributed much to the recording on canvas of a wide range of vessels; private and commercial, naval and merchant, sail and steam. The largest public collection of his work can be seen in the Musée de la Marine in Paris. Although working very much in the ship-portrait tradition, Edouard Adam did attempt variations on the strict broadside composition by sometimes showing vessels from a three-quarter viewpoint, with a vessel under reduced canvas in heavy seas. A particularly good example of the latter is that showing the American Down-Easter *Parthia*, 1891, in a gale, and housed in the Bath Marine Museum, Maine. The ship is shown running under storm jib, fore course and lower topsails. It clearly shows Adam's knowledge of ships, but interestingly he shows the

THE BARQUE *MARYANNE JOHNSTONE* WITH THE TUG *RAMBLER*
Joseph Heard (1799–1859)
N.R. Omell Galleries, London
Another excellent example from this Liverpool-based artist, but this time showing a sailing ship hove-to. This makes a pleasing change from the geometrical shapes usually employed to represent the sails, although they have not been painted in such sharp focus when compared to the hull, giving an almost unfinished quality to the painting. The composition is unusual for a ship portrait in that the artist has shown the tug in front of the main subject, but it does make for an interesting and more active image.

buntlines as nothing more than lines on the sails, and with no running part at all. Nevertheless, it is the detail of the deck layout which is so invaluable to historians, for enough is shown to give an indication of its design and colour scheme.

Although many of the vast number of surviving paintings have signatures, sometimes very little is known about the lives of the artists. This is true of Richard B. Spencer and F. Tudgay, who both flourished between 1850 and 1880. Their work is widely reproduced in studies of mid 19th-century shipbuilding, thanks to the large number of works produced by each on the many famous vessels of the time – vessels often ignored by those considered to be true fine artists. The quality of their work as ship portraits and the accuracy of detail varies considerably, so that some caution is called for when looking at them in a historical context.

T. G. Dutton

Thomas Goldsworthy Dutton, briefly introduced in Chapter Five, on the 19th century in Britain and Europe, was another artist who emphasized accuracy in his ship portraits and whose work is rightly considered to be representative of the finest of the 19th-century lithographers. He was also one of the most prolific, and because of this he is more widely reproduced than Spencer or Tudgay; his excellent version of the final moments of the Great Tea Race of 1866, between the beautiful clipper ships *Ariel* and *Taeping*, must rank as one of the highest.

Dutton worked from a small studio in Fleet Street, London, producing lithographs from his own watercolour originals from about 1850 onwards, which was extremely fortunate for everyone who appreciates the beauty of the British and American clipper ships of the 1850s and 1860s. Although correctly considered a ship-portrait painter, Dutton's work lacks the rigidity and formula found in the works of so many of his peers. There is often an attempt, usually very successfully accomplished, to add greater feeling and activity to his ships and compositions. His drawing ability was also quite exceptional when compared to that of others; not only did Dutton fully understand the technicalities of his chosen subjects, but he was also able to convey convincingly one of the most difficult aspects of marine painting, the way in which a ship sits in the water. Furthermore, he used his drawing ability to great effect in making subtle changes to the angles at which he placed ships in relation to the viewer, and the set of the sails is compatible with the state of the sea, rather than placing every scene set in a Force 8 or 9 gale.

The National Maritime Museum in Greenwich has over the years managed to acquire an almost complete set of his lithographs, including a number of his watercolours, and we must hope that before too long a major retrospective exhibition will be organized to allow these works to be seen by a wider audience. (Sadly, many of the works reproduced in this book and which belong to major national collections are rarely placed on public view). Dutton died in Clapham, South London, in 1891, and, considering his not insubstantial output, he left a comparatively small estate to his long-standing servant.

A Chinese "School"

In some studies the ship-portrait painters are often grouped together as belonging to a "school". This is usually done for convenience rather than because of any underlying trend, because no identifiable style is present, beyond the loose parameters defined here, and, significantly, the concept further extends beyond international boundaries. A more specialized and in-depth study of ship-portrait painters would reveal characteristics which allow for national and regional styles to be identified. An exception to the lack of a clearly identifiable school for a group of painters specializing in this form of marine painting must be the anonymous Chinese artists who were chiefly active during the height of the East India Company and the tea trades of the 19th century, whose work shows similarity in style and interpretation. This identifiable style lies primarily in the composition and the technique of rendering the sea.

Invariably the subject was a named sailing ship, but the occasional steamer or Chinese junk might also be used as the focal point or principal subject, drawn as a true side elevation, and often showing the starboard side. The sails would usually be set on the starboard tack, neatly drawn and with a uniform curvature, with not even a cast shadow from one mast to another, so that nothing would detract the eye from the geometrical shape of the ship's rig. The ship would be flying her national colours as well as her correct signal hoist, with sometimes the owner's house flag too. The sea was shown in one of two basic formats: either a moderate sea with no white caps, or a flat calm, if the ship was at anchor with the sails neatly furled. In the latter case, the technique was often to lay a number of flat, soft-edged base colours, and then overpaint with numerous horizontal lines to represent ripples and an attempt at movement. Reflections were rarely used, except for a combined shadow and reflection immediately under the bows, which, while strictly speaking not accurate, did give an effect which worked in the context of the style of painting as a whole. Common to both the moderate sea and the flat calm would be that most distinctive of features which so often readily identifies a ship portrait from the Chinese "school" – the horizontal band of strong shadow lying across the water in the immediate foreground, with a lighter shadow band lying horizontally below the ship's waterline. In both cases these bands of shadow extend from left to right on the painting. The understanding of tone values was extremely poor, for the detail and clarity of many of these paintings is lost when they are reproduced in black and white – something often missed by art historians. In colour their full beauty can be appreciated.

Naturally, variations on all the above exist, but there is no doubt that during the 1850s, 1860s and 1870s this technique was widely adopted. Examples of the Chinese "school" can be seen in major collections in all those countries who traded with China during the years mentioned, in particular Great Britain and North America.

Of course ships trading to China were not restricted to Hong Kong, as is sometimes imagined, but included, among others, the ports of Canton, Foochow and Shanghai, the entrances of which were sometimes used for the background to these paintings. Regardless of which port they worked from, and bearing in mind the distances between them, the style and technique described above are recognizable. There are also many similarities between these Chinese paintings and those of similar ships by European ship-portrait painters produced at the same time. Although we do not know exactly how the Chinese became influenced by the English "school", it is reasonable to suppose that the style was brought into the Far East by some of the many Chinese who signed on as crew members for the long haul back to England and Europe. This is a more acceptable

THE BRITISH BARQUE *WANDERING CHIEF*; J. BROWN, MASTER
Marie-Edouard Adam (1847–1929)
N.R. Omell Galleries, London
This painting is what many non-specialists consider to be a typical marine artist's representation of the late-19th-century merchant sailing ship.

◁ **THE SCHOONER YACHT *ACTAEA* OF THE EASTERN YACHT CLUB**
Marie-Edouard Adam (1847–1929)
N.R. Omell Galleries, London
Adam was an accomplished ship-portrait painter working from Le Havre, and this example and that above are typical of his direct style and finish.

supposition than that the influence was spread by English artists resident in China.

Sometimes, in order to have paintings ready for a ship's arrival at a port, the artist prepared the sea, sky and background in advance and only included the ship once she was settled at anchor or alongside. This allowed the artist to delineate the shape and details of the vessel correctly. He would then proceed out to the ship in the hope of negotiating a fee with the master or others. Naturally, when one was selling paintings of ships to those who spent much of their lives on them, the detail had to be accurate and seamanlike, apart from any atmospheric effect, and any examination of these paintings will reveal how carefully applied it is. Unfortunately no records exist to indicate whether the Chinese artists actually knew anything about the principles of a European sailing ship's rig, or whether they relied solely on copying from life; if the latter, it says much about their concentration and powers of observation. Obviously those who bought these paintings were satisfied with the prices agreed, because many of them found their way into the homes of seafaring families in both Europe and North America.

There was another little-known outlet for those engaged in the portraying of ships. With the increase in world trade and the expansion of influence of the colonial powers during and after the middle of the 19th century, there developed a natural desire on the part of the educated classes to know what was happening elsewhere. This resulted in the introduction of such illustrated journals and magazines as *The Illustrated London News*, which became increasingly popular and which relied very much on artists who would supply suitable material to accompany the esoteric and verbose reports. Artists prepared drawings or watercolours, some of which were sketched on site, and these were then copied and engraved for inclusion in the magazines. The same process was used when illustrations were required for books, and it is often possible to recognize and identify the origins of some of the works of the more notable marine artists in this engraved form. The work of Dutton is a good example, as many of his works were reproduced in this way.

REUBEN CHAPPELL

A ship-portrait painter who spans the 19th and 20th centuries was Reuben Chappell, born at Hook, near Goole, in Yorkshire in 1870, who was brought up in close proximity to the ships which carried the coal trade from this small inland port. The nature and location of the port also brought Chappell into contact with many of the local and traditional craft which frequented the coastal seas of north-eastern England, the study of which benefited him in his future career. After an apprenticeship with a photographer, during which time he taught himself to paint, he managed to support himself successfully as a marine artist by the time he had reached the age of 20. He was extremely prolific and may have produced more than 12,000 paintings. Because of health problems he moved in 1904 to Par in Cornwall, and remained active there until a stroke in 1924, which affected his eyesight, severely curtailed his output. He died in Cornwall in 1940. The Marstal Ship Museum in Denmark has the largest collection of his works.

Although he worked in oils and gouache (opaque, water-based colour), Chappell's principal medium was watercolour, and he often included the name of the vessel, the port of registration and sometimes the name of the captain at the foot of a painting. He used the knowledge he acquired from his numerous trips afloat to enhance the accuracy of his paintings, and while his works lack the highly finished quality of many others, they are none the less worthy examples of the craft. His greatest difficulty appears to have been in the rendering and effective representation of the sea, and surprisingly his most successful works seem to be those completed in oils. The National Maritime Museum in Greenwich has, among others, an oil painting called simply *The Humber Keel "Harry"*, which shows a more competently painted sea than will be found in many of his watercolours. There are also examples which show that he had a reasonably well-developed sense of colour; many of his studies have been completed with a limited palette, which greatly improves them as visual images. Whether sail or steam, Chappell's vessels are always shown in broadside with the vessel slightly heeling towards the viewer so that some of the deck detail is visible; this is invariably picked out with a holding line, which increases the contrast between the vessel and the surrounding sea and sky. The detail on the hulls and the accuracy of the rigs make Chappell's work useful in establishing the appearance of a vessel at a particular time in her career.

Chappell's use of the name of ship and other details related to the ownership of the vessel is almost peculiar to this type of marine painting. On the European continent, where ship portraiture possibly reached a far more advanced level of development than anywhere else, the application of these details as a title was more widespread. In many case they were often included as a separate band of black running along the bottom edge, with a thin dividing line between the painting proper and the title, which comprised the ship's name, port of registry, captain and port where painted, all picked out in white or deep yellow. The titling was always hand-drawn and often beautifully rendered, either in script or based on a print face.

Reuben Chappell was effectively the last of the genuine British ship-portrait painters who survived entirely by the artistic skill of his own hand. His works represent the ultimate development of an important element in the history of marine painting and, because of the sheer number of coastal vessels he painted, form an important historical collection.

JACOBSEN

Spanning the 19th and 20th centuries, as well as linking the New World with the Old, was Antonio Nicolo Gasparo Jacobsen. He was also considered one of the most successful and prolific of all ship-portrait painters to have established themselves in North America. Born in Denmark in 1850, Jacobsen was trained in painting at the Copenhagen Academy before emigrating to New York in 1871. His first employment was with a safemaker, painting marine views on the doors of safes being sold to shipping companies.

Jacobsen was encouraged to take up ship portraiture by an employee from the Old Dominion Line, based in New York, who also helped him with his early commissions, which he executed from his studio in the suburb of West Hoboken. At the time New York was a lively and thriving port, and it provided him with a wide array of subject-matter, from the small pilot schooners to the impressive transatlantic sailing packets and, more importantly, the steamers, both ocean-going and those which plied the Hudson River. It was his extensive work portraying the numerous steamers calling in at New York which established his fame and reputation. If seen singly, his work has a certain appeal, but when seen as a collection his over-developed formula in painting the sea and sky becomes monotonous and dull. It has been suggested that the formula was indeed deliberate, as he prepared a number of canvases with seas and skies already finished and well in advance of any commissions, very much on the lines of the method of the Chinese artists I have described. As soon as a new vessel had berthed he would sketch what information and details were required for the portrait, and then race home on his horse to complete the painting. When one considers his output and the average size of his canvases, this story does not seem quite so far-fetched. Even a cursory examination of much of Jacobsen's work will reveal the sameness which exists in his seas, and often there appears to be a mismatch between the ship and the sea, although at times the ship can appear part of and sitting in the water.

He was also known to use shipbuilders' draughts to produce images of ships he had never seen, or was not likely to see – something which many historical marine artists of today do as a matter of necessity. On such occasions he would sometimes be assisted by his wife and daughter. His vessels also appear very stiff and without much form or depth, whether he heeled the vessel over towards the viewer or changed from a broadside to a three-quarter view. Some of those vessels viewed from slightly above the horizon line appear almost to be models, often set in seas more akin to those of Cape Horn than the North Atlantic. In all cases the detail was carefully applied, with some fine brushwork and strong use of cast shadows, which give some of his paintings of smaller steamers an almost photographic effect, especially when reproduced in monochrome.

A FULL-RIGGED SHIP UNDER SHORTENED SAIL, IN 1905
Lai Fong of Calcutta (*fl.* 1890–1910)
Christie's, London

Originally from Hong Kong, Lai Fong moved to Calcutta and spent most of his active life as a ship-portrait painter producing work such as this of the large sailing ships which loaded at Bombay. His work is variable; this is of average quality, but nevertheless typical of the almost separate industry which grew in China to satisfy the demands of captains and crew requiring reasonably accurate portraits of their ships. Compare this with the previous examples of ship portraits reproduced in this book, and those which could also be similarly described from the 20th century. The ship herself has not been identified, although the letters "ZMS" are clearly marked along her bow. It is possible that she represents one of the many coolie ships – vessels employed solely to transport cheap labour around the many outposts of the British Empire – for her design is typical of the type, and they were a regular sight at Calcutta.

As I have said, Jacobsen occasionally introduced a change into his compositions, and the Peabody Museum of Salem, Massachusetts, holds a number which demonstrate that if he had put his mind to it, he was capable of producing some interesting and appealing work. Two examples are a painting of the American steamer *Horatio Hall* (1898), and one showing four steamers: the *Herman Winter* (1886), the *H. F. Dimock* (1884), the *Gent'l Whitney* (1873) and the *Old Dominion* (1872). The vessels in both paintings are all American, and the paintings were done in 1916 and 1914 respectively. The first shows the steamer from the starboard bow quarter heading out to sea, with one of the towers of the Brooklyn Suspension Bridge in the left background. As may be expected in a work by Jacobsen, the steamer is very accurately drawn, and even includes the starboard anchor, ready to let go in case of an emergency. The sea is also more subdued, possibly because it would have been noticed by even the most uninitiated. The composition is marred only by the low-lying warehouse to the right background which, even if factually correct, would have benefited from some artistic licence. The second painting, showing the four steamers together, is of exceptional interest because of the number of vessels, even though their relative positions would contravene all international rules on safety at sea. It may be reasonable to assume that this painting was a commission, and that Jacobsen was obliged to show these named vessels together. Again, the vessels are clearly and accurately defined, sitting in a less turbulent sea, and the whole is a composition which gives the impression of more space and depth than is usual in a work by this artist.

The years from 1850 to 1920 might be called the golden age of ship potraiture, and these years coincide with the greatest expansion of trade by sea that the world had ever known. The pace with which this trade grew generated an intensive shipbuilding programme for all types of vessels, both sail and steam. Along with agriculture, the sea provided and created a living for many people, and this enormous job market was not just for those actively employed at sea, but also in associated jobs ashore, in offices and in all the ports and harbours around the coasts. A large number of people from all the social backgrounds which made up this workforce wanted comparatively inexpensive pictures of the ships they knew so well, and this provided another source of employment for those with even basic drawing and painting skills. Thus were created the generations of artists from every seafaring country involved in international trade who, for the most part, remain anonymous and unrecognized, but whose work is not only far more widespread, but has possibly more direct links with the sea than is the case with any other aspect of the history of marine painting.

THE BRITISH BARQUE *LANCASHIRE;* CAPTAIN A EVANS
Lai Fong of Calcutta (*fl.* 1890–1910)
Christie's, London
This is a greatly superior example of Lai Fong's work and is also more typical of his style and technique. Within the sub-specialism of ship-portrait painting, this possibly epitomizes the genre, for it has a quality which conforms to the more widely accepted notion of what marine painting is or should be about.

CHAPTER SEVEN

The 20th Century 1880–1960

THE END OF ONE CENTURY AND THE START OF ANOTHER ARE obviously clearly defined, but there was no such perceptible change in the development of marine painting in Western Europe and North America at the beginning of the 20th century. That social and technological changes were taking place is undeniable, but they were at the same gradual and almost leisurely pace as they had been 10 or 20 years before. Admittedly, at sea, changes were possibly proceeding at a faster pace, as a result of the need for improved communications and the speedy delivery of goods. Deep-water sail was in noticeable decline; the last large, ocean-going, square-rigged sailing ship to be built in Great Britain, the four-masted barque *Archibald Russell*, was constructed in 1905, only one year before the completion of the world's first big-gun, turbine-powered battleship, HMS *Dreadnought*, in 1906. The contrasts in technology between the two were extreme. But commercial sail did continue to provide a substantial source of inspiration for marine artists for many years to come, and, as a specific area within the genre, the subject of the sailing ship reached perhaps its highest levels during the first half of this century.

As with the Suez Canal in 1869, the opening of the Panama Canal in 1914 contributed to the decline in sail tonnage, especially for those ships employed in the South American nitrate trade. Companies such as the famous F. Laiesz from Hamburg and A. D. Bordes of Nantes, with their beautifully powerful four- and five-masted sailing ships, did manage to continue for a few years after 1918. But it was Gustaf Erickson of Mariehamn in Åland who was destined to be the last owner of a fleet of commercial, cargo-carrying sailing ships. Some of the maritime museums in Germany, France, Finland and, to a lesser extent, from other north European countries who supplied crews for Erickson's ships, contain marvellous professional and amateur examples of how the ships of these three owners dominated the range of some marine artists' output.

JOHANNES HOLST

One marine artist who tended to concentrate on paintings of the last of the large, cargo-carrying sailing ships was the German Johannes Holst (1880–1965). Unfortunately he is little known and reproduced outside his country of birth; his work deserves a wider public. As with so many artists, his early work can at times lack impact, although he always succeeded in painting the sea with great conviction. As his career progressed, so did his ability, and one of his most redeeming qualities was that he invariably places his ships in a broad expanse of sea and sky, rather than making the sea only secondary and incidental – a fault with so many marine artists. Often the ships were depicted under reduced sail, with a heavy sea running, but the whole composition was well-balanced, with a controlled palette – an approach to marine painting adopted by many artists in Germany, such as Robert Schmidt-Hamburg (1885–1963), although lack of published evidence makes it difficult to ascertain whether this was due to Holst's influence. He has been criticized for his technique for rendering the sea, because it is very much formula-based. However, this judgement has tended to cloud the opinion of many critics because, as I have said, so little of his work is known outside northern Germany, and his work is very much in need of a reappraisal. Be this as it may, Holst's work epitomizes the final years of the sailing ship.

SPURLING AND DAWSON

Two other, quite diverse marine artists who made a painting career on the subject of commercial sail – especially the clipper ships – were John Robert Charles Spurling (1870–1933), and Montague Dawson (1895–1973), although their work could not be further apart in style, technique or medium. It is unlikely that anyone interested in the history of sail has not heard of or seen reproductions of some of Spurling's ship portraits although it is rarely possible to examine an original because so many were destroyed in the bombing of London during the Second World War, and those which have survived are given little public display. Unlike Holst, who was concerned with the total environment in which his ships are set, Spurling was concerned with an accurate portrayal of the ships themselves. This he carried out with great skill and knowledge, as far as the available reference sources permitted, and also drawing on his own practical experience at sea as a young man. However, Spurling was prone to some fantastic whims of artistic licence when it

THE WHITE STAR LINER *TEUTONIC* LEAVING LIVERPOOL ON HER MAIDEN VOYAGE, AUGUST 1889
William Lionel Wyllie (1851–1931)
National Maritime Museum, London

Wyllie was undoubtedly one of the greatest marine painters of the late 19th and early 20th centuries; he was also prolific in a wide range of media, from pencil and wash drawings to watercolour and oils, including a vast output of etchings. When this is considered, it is remarkable that so few of his works have been reproduced and that no in-depth and fully illustrated study has been published, apart from a monograph of somewhat limited scope. His ability to record the many variations, moods and atmospheres of sea and sky, combined with his superb and sensitive draughtsmanship and his delineation of the complex shapes of ships and other vessels, places his work in the league of the great and universally recognized masters of painting. This painting is but one example of his skill in recording a specific event, but within the context of a carefully observed, controlled and rendered composition which brings the whole canvas to life. It is also representative of Wyllie's ability to control colour and, through a restricted palette, maintain the natural light and subdued colours which were no doubt what he saw in reality as he made his preliminary sketches. One wonders how he would have used his natural skill and ability in recording the vessels of the 17th century had he been alive at the time.

△ HMS *VICTORY* AND OTHER VESSELS IN PORTSMOUTH HARBOUR
Harold Wyllie (1880–1973)
Royal Exchange Art Gallery, London

◁ △ DER VIERMASTBARK
Johannes Holst (1880–1965)
Deutsches Schiffahrtsmuseum, Bremerhaven

◁ ▽ RUNNING FREE
Montague Dawson (1895–1973)
Royal Exchange Art Gallery, London

came to the inclusion of cast shadows across sails and hulls. In some cases these shadows have no bearing on the relationship of the sun's position, or indeed the time of day. There are also one or two gross errors of drawing in the construction of some of the hulls. But there can be no doubt that his watercolour and gouache studies of sailing ships, with their intricate tracery of rigging, will have an appeal for at least as long as there remain admirers of this past technology. In many respects, and if Spurling's work is examined as marine art first and for its subject second, he can be considered the 20th-century equivalent of the Roux family (see Chapters Four and Five).

Montague Dawson, on the other hand, could be said to link the concepts of Holst with those of Spurling; he attempted to portray his ships in the open sea with sufficient detail for the expert to identify correctly or recognize a named vessel. However, he was not entirely successful, because the formula he developed for painting sailing ships often showed the ship perched on top of a heavy sea, and with every sail set. Dusk and sunrise were also favourite settings, giving rise to some unusual and unnatural reflected light on the sails and hulls, which were themselves often incorrectly proportioned. Unfortunately this formula was developed during the period when Dawson had achieved considerable success as a result of the large number and variety of reproductions of his work which were made available. This has rightly undermined his quality and standing as one of the more notable marine artists of the 20th century, and it is necessary to return to his formative years as an artist to see evidence of a talent which was so sadly misdirected. His earlier works are far more successful, and show that Dawson was capable of producing great pieces beyond the "chocolate-box" image with which his work is now associated.

THE NEW ZEALAND SHIPPING COMPANY'S SHIP *WAIMATE,* 1874
John Robert Charles Spurling (1870–1933)
P & O, London

A 20th-century ship-portrait painter who strove for absolute technical accuracy in his ships, but was prone to much artistic licence in the application of light and shade, Spurling is often scornfully criticized by many marine art historians. This is an injustice and a failure to recognize the contribution of his work to the development of many modern marine artists. This example is one from the vast output of sailing ships he painted during the latter part of his life, and exemplifies his unmistakable technique in painting the sea, sails and shadows. It is a watercolour, heightened with body-colour.

Regardless of the standing of both Spurling or Dawson as marine artists, their work inspired, and continues to inspire, amateurs to the field of marine painting. Many of these deliberate copies or new works resulting from the influences of these two artists actually incorporate the same errors of drawing, light, shadow and composition.

PATTERSON AND GRANT

Charles Robert Patterson's work, while from the other side of the Atlantic, could be said to equate well with that of Dawson. He was born in Southampton in 1878, the son of an owner of a local shipbuilding company, and left England for America in his early 20s. He became not only a very successful and much admired marine artist, concentrating on the history and development of sailing ships under the American flag, but also made a name for himself as a naval historian, writing about the history and careers of specific ships. During the 1920s and 1930s there was much interest in America in the history of their merchant marine, resulting from the publication of a number of excellent books, many of which included reproductions of paintings by Patterson; this undoubtedly helped to enhance his standing among marine artists. Although Patterson strove for accuracy in his paintings, he did not take it to the same extremes as Spurling, and his

THE BRITISH INDIA STEAM NAVIGATION COMPANY'S LINER, THE *BARRABOOL,* 1923
John Robert Charles Spurling (1870–1933)
P & O, London

Spurling completed a number of steamship paintings using the same successful techniques as for his sailing-ship portraits, and this is one of his more highly finished illustrative studies. It is possibly more representative of Spurling's technique than the sailing ship opposite; clearly, technical accuracy and detail were of great interest and importance to him. The contrast between this study of a liner and that by Wyllie which opens this chapter is apparent, and shows two distinct approaches to the subject; both artists achieve their aim successfully, but through completely different methods.

△ THE ORIENT LINER *ORVIETO,* 1908
William Marshall Birchall (1884–*c.* 1935)
P & O, London

▽ WITH A BONE IN HER TEETH
William Marshall Birchall (1884–*c.* 1935)
Royal Exchange Art Gallery, London

THE CUNARD LINER *CAMPANIA* AT ANCHOR IN THE MERSEY
William Marshall Birchall (1884–*c.* 1935)
Peabody Museum of Salem
With economy of detail, and relying much on the eye of the observer, Birchall has effectively captured the design and strange beauty of a typical early-20th-century transatlantic liner. He has controlled the impact and potentially overpowering nature of the famous Cunard red funnels with some skill, to create a balanced, well-observed and neatly sketched watercolour painting. He is another marine artist who sadly remains little known, except by those with a specialist interest in marine painting.

seas are far more naturalistic than those of Dawson's later period, but possibly without the finesse and observational skills of Holst. He died in 1958.

A contemporary of Patterson's who also developed a career as a marine artist around the historical aspects of sail was Gordon Hope Grant, born in San Francisco in 1875. He was the son of a Scots banking official who had nautical connections. His father's wish for his son to be given a Scottish education meant a voyage in a sailing ship around Cape Horn to Scotland, and eventual employment with a Clyde-based shipbuilding company. This was never to be, because Grant's paintings had been noticed by the editor of a London magazine, and he undertook three years of art training in the capital. On completion of this course he returned to America, where he worked for a number of magazines, unitl his move to New York and a journey to South Africa in 1899 to cover the Boer War as an illustrator.

From 1918 onwards, Grant became a full-time marine artist working in watercolours, oils, lithographs and etchings. Like Patterson, he also wrote about things nautical, having at least six books published, and occasionally returned to sea. He became far better known than Patterson and is considered one of the most successful practitioners of marine painting of his time. In comparison to Patterson's work, however, Grant's is loose and lacking in detail, and lacks the overall quality of his peer. He tended to aim more for an effect, and even though he produced many paintings of named ships, they are more representative than accurate historical records. He died in New York in 1962.

The changes at sea, at least until the events leading up to the outbreak of war in 1914 and, to a lesser extent, after, offered a wide variety of subjects from which marine artists could draw. This period perhaps produced more diverse styles, interpretations and variations of themes and specific subjects than any other period in the history of the art form. Some of these interpretations resulted from the influence of the Impressionists, who were predominantly active in France during the second half of the 19th century. The great emphasis of the Impressionists on the recording of contemporary life and experience, combined with their highly developed awareness of the effect of natural light, was also indirectly responsible for the approaches adopted by some of the great marine artists practising during the early years of this century. But, generally speaking, the concept of the imitation of nature, or realism, in the sense that the artist attempted to portray and record what he saw, remained to the fore in mainstream marine painting, and has continued very much so to this day. Even the Post-Impressionist period and the applications of abstract theory in the development of modern art had little effect on marine painting. Naturally, some artists were exceptions, but they tended to work in isolation, and in the terms of this study are of no consequence.

The pictorial evidence of the great 19th-century romantic and powerfully moving marine paintings speaks for itself, but, as stated, the traditions did not falter. Two artists, among many, whose work continued these traditions and which were carried over from the old to the new century, were Julius Olsson and Sir Frank Brangwyn. They were representative rather than exceptions, although both produced some outstanding works, using a common theme but adopting different approaches.

JULIUS OLSSON

Olsson was born in London in 1864, the son of an English mother and a Swedish father. He trained for a career in commerce, but soon left to take up painting and indulge his interest in travel. He was without any formal art training, but still achieved the distinction of having his first work exhibited at the Royal Academy in 1890. In 1896 he moved from London to St Ives in Cornwall, where he remained until 1915, when he returned to London to join the Royal Naval Volunteer Reserve. He continued to live in London until the bombing during the Second World War caused him to move to Dalkey, outside Dublin,

△ KING EDWARD VII CLASS BATTLESHIPS AT SEA, 1912
Alma Claude Burlton Cull (1880–1931)
National Maritime Museum, London
This is possibly the most successful painting of 20th-century warships ever executed. It is an example of marine painting at its best, demonstrating the most important attribute of movement, atmosphere, the correct relationship between sea, sky and apparent weather conditions and, of course, accuracy in the rendering and actions of the ships. The artist achieved in his studies of Royal Navy ships what Somerscales did in his studies of the merchant sailing ship, and if the comparison is taken to include the detail of technique and the capturing of atmosphere, then Cull was perhaps the more highly skilled.

▷ THE SS *CITY OF LONDON* IN THE SUEZ CANAL
Frank William Brangwyn (1867–1956)
Royal Exchange Art Gallery, London
An artist of considerable drawing skill, who could respond to commissions on a wide range and variety of subjects, Brangwyn was also at ease with nautical subjects and able to place them in a composition with a strong human element, as demonstrated here, with his usual highly developed skill.

▷ "C" CLASS BATTLE SQUADRON, 1924
Alma Claude Burlton Cull (1880–1931)
N.R. Omell Galleries, London
Whether painting with oils or watercolours, Cull competes on equal terms with the studies of warships produced by William Lionel Wyllie, especially with the latter's watercolours. Here Cull demonstrates his ability to record and paint accurately what are difficult subjects to capture convincingly in watercolour: a cloudy dusk and the resultant oily and dark, yet moving, sea which this light so often creates.

▽ HMS *REVENGE* ON SUMMER EXERCISES IN THE MEDITERRANEAN IN 1928
Alma Claude Burlton Cull (1880–1931)
Royal Exchange Art Gallery, London
In this example, again a watercolour, the setting and atmosphere are more subdued and peaceful. Even though the subject is one of aggression, in that it portrays warships, Cull has managed to tame it by this sensitive and excellently controlled composition. As usual with Cull's work, his tone control and understanding of light are almost faultless.

where he died in 1942. During his time in Cornwall Olsson quickly established himself as a central figure among the fast-growing community of artists, and it was also in Cornwall that he received the greatest inspiration for many of his works, for which he has become particularly well known. As a marine artist Olsson was very much concerned with the mood of the sea and the sense of loneliness and isolation which it can convey, rather than as a backdrop for recording specific maritime events. And because he concentrated on seascapes, especially moonlit ones, his work can at times be difficult to place. His style of oil painting is very bold and loose; it has been described as a "rather messy Impressionistic technique", which is possibly a reflection on how his work is seen now, for during the height of his very successful career he was highly regarded and achieved the distinction of having his 1911 Royal Academy painting, *Moonlit Shore, near St Ives, Cornwall*, bought by the Chantrey Bequest.

Sir Frank Brangwyn

Brangwyn was a much more diverse artist, whose abilities extended far beyond marine painting, stretching to figure studies, industrial and architectural subjects, among others, using a wide variety of media, from watercolour to oils and including lithography, engraving and frescoes. He was also able to use his skills three-dimensionally, through the design of rooms and furniture. Brangwyn was born in 1867 in Bruges, Belgium, his family having moved there in the belief that life would be less expensive than in London. However, they returned to London in 1875, and from 1880 Brangwyn practised drawing at the Victoria & Albert Museum, also receiving tutorial assistance from his father, who exhibited architectural designs at the Royal Academy on an irregular basis. It was at the V & A that Brangwyn met William Morris, the famous artist, designer, decorator and poet, and as a result he worked at Morris's studio in London between the years 1882 and 1884. Brangwyn's highly developed and natural drawing skill soon brought him recognition, for in 1885 he had his first painting accepted and hung at the Royal Academy. In 1889, thanks to his success, he was able to travel, and thus came into contact with the Parisian Art Nouveau movement, whose influence is apparent in much of his work from this period. He was elected an Associate Royal Academician in 1904 and a full RA in 1919. His knighthood was granted in 1941 in recognition of his services and contribution to British art. Sir Frank Brangwyn died in Sussex, southern England, in 1956, after an enormously successful career.

Brangwyn was not a specialist in the field of marine painting, but the few studies he completed have contri-

HMS *ROYAL SOVEREIGN* ENTERING PORTLAND IN 1928
Alma Claude Burlton Cull (1880–1931)
Royal Exchange Art Gallery, London
Anyone who has experienced the arrival of a warship into this harbour will appreciate the accuracy with which the artist has captured this scene, especially in relation to the overall light effects and the powerful presence of the ship.

REFITTING
Arthur John Trevor Briscoe (1873–1943)
Christie's, London
This etching is typical of the prolific output from this successful and accomplished marine artist. His knowledge of the detail and workings of the large square-rigged sailing ships, combined with his well-developed draughtsmanship, enabled him to compose many sometimes unusual, but always interesting, studies of crew at work.

buted immensely to its development. He used his ability to draw and render the human form to great effect in all his paintings, and particularly in his marines. One of his early marine paintings, *All Hands Shorten Sail* (1889), in the Rochdale Art Gallery, is a beautiful example of the expert composition of a deck scene which accurately conveys the violent movement of a comparatively small sailing vessel caught in a rising wind and sea, with dramatic human activity. The ship is shown from the starboard waist of the main deck, looking aft towards the helmsman, with a member of the crew in the process of hoisting himself into the main shrouds to follow his two companions aloft to take in the sail. The composition is made all the more powerful both by the angle the ship is at, and by the fact that the two crew members already climbing the shrouds are facing forward in anticipation of the effort which will be required to reduce sail sufficiently to prevent a disaster. The ship and her fittings are drawn with an accuracy which suggests that Brangwyn was not unfamiliar with sailing ships, even though he may himself have not experienced such conditions. This accuracy of course gives the painting historical credibility

SS *PESHAWUR,* 1871; LAT 36°21 'N, LONG 8°14 'W
William Lionel Wyllie (1851–1931)
P & O, London
An excellent deck scene from the hand of a great master, showing that Wyllie's interest in marine painting extended to all facets of life at sea and was not restricted to the portrayal of ships. This watercolour also demonstrates his ability to observe and draw the human figure in detail and without the stiffness so often shown by those less talented.

too, although, as with many marine paintings in this book, they were mere interpretations of everyday events at the time they were completed. The painting also works as a whole because of the limited palette; the overall use of slightly green-tinged yellow ochre, raw umber and black help to create the correct light and weather conditions.

Another notable oil painting by Brangwyn which deserves detailed examination is his *The Funeral at Sea: "We Therefore Commit His Body to the Deep"* (1890), now owned by the Glasgow Art Gallery and Museum in Scotland. It shows with clarity and sensitivity the simple service and arrangements employed at sea in the days of sail when a man died. And although this is the subject, Brangwyn does not make an issue of the incident, but it appears almost as if the viewer is one of the crew members, quietly observing the ceremony before continuing with his duties – a break in an existence which was so often event-free that there was little to differentiate one day from the next. Again, there is a good sense of balance in the composition, with a high degree of technical accuracy, all rendered with a limited palette. As with all his work, his knowledge of perspective is excellent.

GREENWICH HOSPITAL
William Lionel Wyllie (1851–1931)
Royal Exchange Art Gallery, London
In the great traditions of the work of the Old Masters, Wyllie here selects a setting which was close to his heart – a busy, thriving and active river in the background of which he places his subject. And although the subject is architectural, there is no doubt that one is looking at a marine painting. He was always able to convey a strong sense of depth and space in his composition of a painting.

A FRIEND OF NATIONS
William Lionel Wyllie (1851–1931)
Royal Exchange Art Gallery, London
This is a beautifully atmospheric oil sketch of a small wooden brig being towed to safety by a wallowing paddle tug. The extremely limited palette, the minimal detail and the carefully controlled light conditions combine to make this seemingly insignificant study a worthy example of the marine artist's skill and of Wyllie's in particular. Note the cormorants skimming the waves to the left of the two vessels. The sea and sky are well observed and capture both movement and weather conditions admirably. Whether as a sketch for a more highly finished painting or as a painting in its own right, a study such as this deserves extended attention, if only for the inspiration it generates.

Both the above paintings and the one reproduced in this book are comparable with the best of the marine paintings which have been bought by the Chantrey Bequest.

ARTHUR BRISCOE

Another artist who excelled at deck scenes with a strong emphasis on the human element was Arthur John Trevor Briscoe (1873–1943). Briscoe was very much a specialist marine painter who acquired a formal art training in oils, watercolours and etching at the Slade School in London, and at the Académie Julian in Paris. Briscoe's early commissions were illustrating books and producing cartoons for magazines, although his background gave him a certain financial independence, so that, unlike many other young unknown artists at the time, he did not have to rely too much on this type of work before being able to devote himself more fully to marine subjects. Briscoe had a good eye and a talent for pure drawing which he used to achieve a number of beautiful and sensitively controlled watercolours, and a vast output of carefully observed etchings, for which he was and is particularly well known. He also had extensive experience as a yachtsman, and made a number of short trips in

STORM AND SUNSHINE, A BATTLE WITH THE ELEMENTS
William Lionel Wyllie (1851–1931)
National Maritime Museum, London
This painting is in the same league as Wyllie's famous masteriece, *Toil, glitter, grime and wealth on a flowing tide,* which was purchased through the Chantrey Bequest and which unfortunately could not be reproduced in this book. The dramatic scene above shows the powder hulk *Leonidas* in the river Medway during a heavy squall, with the sun reflecting off the hull as it finds a gap in the storm-laden clouds. It is a powerfully moving image and contains many carefully observed details, which all contribute to its effectiveness and impact. This is one of at least two paintings of this hulk which Wyllie completed, and although the other is equally competent, this is by far the more dramatic.

coasters and small sailing vessels, putting the knowledge he so acquired to good use in his work. He exhibited at the Royal Academy, but did not achieve ARA or RA status, although in 1930, not surprisingly, he was elected a member of the Royal Society of Painters, Etchers and Engravers, known less cumbersomely as the RE.

ANTON OTTO FISCHER

The traditions being gradually established and the continued development of a separate North American School of marine painting during the early part of this century can be illustrated through the life and work of Anton Otto Fischer, because, although a German by birth, he was never directly influenced by European trends. Fischer was born into poverty in Munich in 1882 and became an orphan soon after. Although he had no connections with the sea, he went to Hamburg and thence to sea, serving in a variety of craft until in 1903, as a deckhand on board the British barque *Gwydyr Castle*, he landed in New York, where he decided to stay, gaining employment by crewing on yachts and instructing in seamanship on a local school ship. He soon found work with Arthur Frost, the painter and illustrator, and when the Frost family

moved back to France in 1906 Fischer decided that he too was going to follow a career as an artist. From money he had saved he went to Paris and enrolled at the Académie Julian, only just missing his contemporary, Arthur Briscoe. Returning in 1906 to New York, his adopted home, he quickly established himself as a painter and illustrator, though not necessarily devoted to marine subjects. In the next six years he became well known and successful, acquiring a reputation for the quality of his illustrations of Jack London's stories. Fischer became an American citizen in 1916 and his career never seems to have suffered as a result of his German birth, for soon after the First World War he became one of America's most sought-after illustrators, known in wider circles for his extensive work for the *Tug Boat Annie* series and the *Saturday Evening Post*. The demands of his illustration commissions meant that it was some time before he was able to devote himself more fully to marine painting, often with a strong human element. He remained active until his death in 1962.

Fischer was particularly proud of his American citizenship, as is demonstrated in a photograph of him wearing the uniform of a lieutenant-commander of the United States Coast Guard, in which he was commis-

THE DIAMOND JUBILEE FLEET REVIEW OF 1897
William Lionel Wyllie (1851–1931)
N.R. Omell Galleries, London

sioned during the Second World War, although, much to his regret, he made only one cruise on active service. This involvement in the USCG was the result of Fischer's commission to produce a number of paintings for them; it allowed him more direct access to obtain references for his paintings without having to be too concerned about security and identification.

The appeal of Fischer's work contrasts quite considerably with that of the work of Briscoe or of the few marines by Brangwyn; both these artists used the human element as a basis for much of their output. In one respect the contrast demonstrates the more natural flair at drawing the human form of both Briscoe and Brangwyn. Fischer was also prone on occasions to use a wider palette range, which can give some paintings an almost amateurish effect. However, when he did limit himself the effect is far more realistic and atmospheric.

An example of the former is his interpretation of the action between the *Bon Homme Richard* and the *Serapis*, north of Flamborough Head in 1779. It shows the two vessels engaged in close combat at night or at dusk, the focal point being the intense white light generated by the fire and possible explosions on board one of the ships. The sails and sea are all filled with purple and bright yellow, reflecting the fires, while the sky is an intense blue. The whole is extremely colourful, with little colour balance between the three components of the painting – the ships, the sea and the sky – which unfortunately all combine to detract from the nature of the subject.

An example of a muted palette, and therefore a more satisfying and realistic image, is found in his painting, *A Tanker in Heavy Seas*. The basic colour is a very subdued and soft warm grey, which works effectively in conveying the impression of a tanker ploughing across a heavy broadside sea, with an equally strong wind blowing. The tanker herself is almost confined in appearance to her silhouette, the detail being obscured by the spray and foam-filled air. There are of course many other examples of both extremes from this artist's work and one wonders whether he himself was ever aware of the divergent nature of his art.

Besides these variations in colour application, there appear at times some rather disturbing drawing errors indicative of Fischer's problems with complex perspective and its application when determining proportions. In Fischer's defence, however, it is fair to say that the ship, especially the square-rigged sailing ship, is probably the most difficult to draw with absolute conviction, as it is made up of so many compound curves. When this problem is mastered, the next is to place it convincingly on and in the sea, something already discussed in this study. Generally speaking, though, Fischer's work is the forerunner of the superb style and approach being adopted by marine artists in North America today – very much illustrative in content, and with a strong emphasis on detail and realism.

GEORGE CANNING WALES

An American-born marine draughtsman and illustrator whose work reflects the development of the American scene during the first half of this century more truly than that of Fischer is George Canning Wales (1868–1940). Besides his contribution to the work of that most distinguished of American maritime historians, Howard I. Chappelle, *The History of American Sailing Ships*, first published in 1935, he is not widely known. In this particular book Wales's major involvement was in the production of measured perspectives of the hulls used to illustrate American sailing-ship development. These clear, concise and accurate drawings are a testament to Wales's experience, training and abilities as a draughtsman, although they should more correctly be referred to as technical illustrations. Within the more traditional understanding of marine painting, Wales's work is very precise and confident. The Peabody Museum of Salem, Massachusetts, has a number of his watercolour paintings and pencil-and-wash drawings which show the lengths to which he went in order to achieve accuracy. As working drawings, some are not only technically highly accurate,

THE P & O LINER *ORSOVA* AT ADEN

Charles Pears (1873–1958)

P & O, London

Pears developed one of the most unusual, but invariably effective, methods of depicting the sea to be used by a marine artist, and this is an example of that technique. It demands a particularly highly developed level of draughtsmanship, especially since it relies very much on an almost geometrical approach, in a similar vein to that used by an earlier master, Canaletto. It also shows the method he adopted in painting his ships; tight, accurate and very illustrative in style.

◁ △ THE SURRENDER OF U-BOAT *U3* TO THE TRAWLER *LADY SHIRLEY*, 7 DECEMBER 1941
Charles Pears (1873–1958)
National Maritime Museum, London
At first glance this painting conveys the impression of a simple, easy technique when, in fact, it is heavily dependent on Pear's drawing skills and his ability to apply the right colour and tonal balance.

◁ A BATTLESHIP OF THE *QUEEN ELIZABETH* CLASS
Charles Pears (1873–1958)
National Maritime Museum, London
This equally excellent painting shows Pears' earlier techniques. Although the sea may conform to more traditional methods used by marine painters (but with a hint of his future geometrical approach just coming to the surface) the ships remain tightly drawn and carefully painted, with just enough detail for the observer to understand shape and form.

HEAVY WEATHER IN THE CHANNEL; STOWING THE MAINSAIL
Frank William Brangwyn (1867–1956)
National Maritime Museum, London
A masterpiece of sympathetic and careful observation which sums up the concept of man's eternal struggle against the forces of the sea and weather during the last days of the merchant sailing ship.

but extremely beautiful and satisfying as images in their own right, and are excellent examples of pure drawing, regardless of the subject-matter. The quality is such that it would be a valuable and worthwhile exercise for some of his sketchbooks to be reproduced in full, making his work available to a wider audience.

Charles J. A. Wilson (1880–1965) is another American artist and illustrator in very much the same mould as Wales. He worked in a wide variety of media, including pencil, pen-and-ink, watercolour, gouache and oil. His draughtsmanship, while not consistently up to Wales's standard, is nevertheless extremely commendable, especially when applied to drawings and paintings of steam vessels. Again, the Peabody Museum has examples of his work.

THE WAR ARTISTS

This study of marine painting has shown the impact of wars and campaigns on the subject-matter available to artists specializing in the genre. The two World Wars of the 20th century, and indeed the more isolated wars which have continued almost unabated as well, all continue to generate visual images of widely varying quality. In Chapter Six reference was made to the early line engravings used to illustrate magazines such as *The Illustrated London News*. These magazines brought home to their readers events happening around the world, not the least important being the developments in the naval arms race between the major powers before the First World War. As printing technology improved with the widespread introduction of the screened half-tone, so young and established artists were able to have their work reproduced without having to go through an engraver. This also speeded up the process by which images sketched on site could be printed, reducing the time delay between the actual event and when the readers were informed about it. This improvement, combined with the public's increasing desire for information and news, was used to good effect in both World Wars – and, of course, before and after – and many artists benefited from the opportunities offered, including the chance to travel to fulfil the requirements of a commission.

Some marine artists were employed by the magazines, others, in an official capacity, by the government as war artists. Of course, as previously mentioned, the activity of artists was not restricted to periods of war, and many artists supplemented their income from painting by also working for magazines, including, as evidenced by Anton Fischer, books and magazines of a more general nature. William Lionel Wyllie (1851–1931), Norman Wilkinson (1878–1971) and Charles Pears (1873–1958) are among the outstanding marine artists of the 20th century who regularly contributed to *The Illustrated London News*, *Sphere* and *Graphic*. Any cursory examination of this

A CROSS-CHANNEL PACKET STEAMSHIP
Norman Wilkinson (1878–1971)
National Maritime Museum, London
This famous marine artist is usually associated with the collection of paintings he completed on the war at sea during the Second World War, rather than the more peaceful and relaxed image portrayed here, and yet this is more in keeping with his vast output in a long and active career. He was fond of applying the oil paint thickly, and of relying very much on the subconscious to delineate detail and, in some cases, shapes.

△ THE P & O LINER *STRATHEDEN* OFF PORT SAID

Norman Wilkinson (1878–1971)

P & O, London

A colourful and more detailed example from the brush of this prolific artist. Although it is what might be termed a "cheerful" study, the wide range of colours used possibly makes this more appropriate as an illustration for a poster, and it allows an interesting comparative study with the painting on the left; two very different, yet effective, impressions of ships at sea in different conditions and for different viewers.

◁ A RESCUE TUG APPROACHING A STEAMSHIP

Norman Wilkinson (1878–1971)

National Maritime Museum, London

This is one of the series of paintings of the naval war which Wilkinson completed. Many of these paintings, which he donated to the British nation, would be more appropriate in an action comic, for they tend to lack the necessary finesse apparent in the work of many other marine artists who recorded naval actions. Wilkinson's paintings are also too subjective, because they are too patriotic. However, the example on the left is one of his better pieces and shows that he was capable of producing a marine painting of a wartime incident with subtlety and understanding. It also demonstrates his appreciation of the beautiful light conditions so often only apparent at sea, and their effect on both the sea and any ships which might be in the vicinity.

HMS *SOUTHAMPTON* ON THE MORNING OF THE BATTLE OF JUTLAND, 31 MAY 1916
Oscar Parkes (1885–1958)
National Maritime Museum, London
Originally a naval surgeon, Parkes eventually became well known as a highly respected historian, specializing in the technical design and development of the battleship. His extensive knowledge extended to other classes of warships which were in commission during his life, especially between the two World Wars. Marine painting appears to have been an extension to his interests and, as this oil painting shows, he became an accomplished practitioner.

illustrative work in comparison to their mainstream painting is very revealing about their individual development and progression, but it is an area often neglected in studies on marine painting. In the majority of cases, these artists did not continue their association with these magazines on a regular basis once they had been able to establish themselves and were receiving a steady flow of commissions. In fact there were some artists – who should more correctly be called illustrators – whose professional life was spent concentrating on this type of work, and whose paintings were only secondary.

However, the work thus produced offers a good insight into natural drawing abilities because the artists had little or no time to rework their sketches or over-paint, should they not be happy with some aspect or other. These illustrations were often produced on site and reflect the spontaneity of the artists' notes and sketchbooks, which unfortunately are rarely reproduced. The combined restrictions of colour printing technology and costs meant that the illustrations (more commonly referred to as wash drawings), were produced in monochrome, using either a black-and-white or a brown-and-white, and in some cases a blue-and-white, base. By rendering the illustration in the first instance in monochrome, the artist

THE CUNARD LINER *MAURETANIA* INBOUND
George Canning Wales (1868–1940)
Peabody Museum of Salem
This delicate and well-drawn sketch has not been reproduced the wrong way around; it is in fact a study for an etching. The simplicity of line and monochrome wash are beautifully subtle, and yet the movement of the swell and the passing liner give a sense of life. Wales preferred pencil drawing, with occasional light and transparent watercolour washes overlaid on top. His draughtsmanship is always carefully controlled, and he went to considerable lengths to ensure that his ships were technically accurate, detailed and correctly proportioned.

had a greater degree of control over contrast and tone values, and the printed image lost nothing in clarity or detail. Nevertheless a number of artists executed what at first appear to be excellent and outstanding paintings, but on reproduction in black-and-white they appear flat, lacking in depth and contrast and generally not very inspiring. It is often too easy to rely on colour to differentiate, while working in monochrome requires more thought if the total image is to work successfully.

Those who were employed as official war artists were not restricted to working in monochrome, but were able to work very much as they had done in peacetime. There were often useful and beneficial perks which went with being an official war artist, not the least being access to areas and events restricted to the public. Many received temporary commissions within either the regular services or one of the variations of the reserves, sometimes attaining quite senior positions. Norman Wilkinson, for example, after a period on active service in the Royal Naval Reserve developed the concept of dazzle painting (bold form of geometrical camouflage), which was widely adopted by the Allies during the later stages of the First World War. He left the Royal Navy with the rank of lieutenant-commander in 1918, but was back in uniform

The Pool

△ THE POOL OF LONDON
Charles Dixon (1872–1934)
Royal Exchange Art Gallery, London
A scene from which Dixon acquired immense inspiration, and well suited to his spontaneous use of watercolour. The composition is excellent, with the comparatively empty area of river midstream leading the eye towards Tower Bridge in the background, and yet the activity of sail and steam on each side is not ignored. The subdued colours well reflecting the industrial and grimy nature of the location in 1901, are typical of Dixon's understanding and appreciation of atmosphere.

◁ OFF SOUTHSEA, 1902
Charles Dixon (1872–1934)
Royal Exchange Art Gallery, London
In complete contrast Dixon has here captured the bright open aspect of the approach to the naval base at Portsmouth, with Southsea beach to the left and the Isle of Wight in the distance on the right, as a Royal Sovereign class battleship approaches. This quick sketch, which may have been a study for a later painting, is again beautifully composed. His observational drawing skill was highly developed, and he was always able to record the essence of a ship's proportions without having to rely on meticulous detail.

for the Second World War, this time with the Royal Air Force as air commodore responsible for camouflage.

The practice of appointing war artists did not arise through the First World War, but had been loosely established during the Crimean and Boer Wars of the 19th and early 20th centuries. It was, however, put onto a more formal and regulated footing during the course of 1916 under the government minister Charles F. G. Masterman, at Wellington House in London. Although illustrations and paintings were used to supplement the written and photographic output of the government's propaganda machine, the Department of Information, the underlying reason for the introduction of professional artists' work in support of the war effort was the lack of official photographers on the Western Front. Furthermore, the subject of trench warfare was far in excess of its ability to provide new inspiration and it was felt, by Masterman himself, that artists would be more able to create images which would capture and inspire the imagination of the public. The new and improved printing techniques also allowed reproductions to be made relatively cheaply, bringing the work of the artists to a wider audience.

Those artists employed to record events at sea came under the auspices of the Admiralty; a special sub-

THE TSS *ROTORUA*
Charles Dixon (1872–1934)
P & O, London
The composition of this ship portrait is dominated by the liner, making the sky and sea completely secondary, although the two small sailing craft in the foreground give the whole painting movement and life.

committee was convened to oversee the work and maintain some sort of effective organization. Interestingly, the marine and naval works produced for the nation under the war artist scheme are more comprehensive as a collection representing the whole spectrum of the war than those for the Army and Air Forces. This was in part due to the fact that the Royal Navy personnel managing the artists had a genuine interest in art. The overriding aim of the Admiralty sub-committee was to record "every Branch of the British Navy with regard to types of ships, bases and areas involved in naval operations". Although it was formally in operation only from December 1917, its aim was achieved, and the majority of the paintings and drawings now reside in the Imperial War Museum, London, which since its foundation in 1917, generated its own collection of war paintings alongside the official ones from the Department of Information. Before 1917, the war at sea was recorded by marine artists sent on location by magazines and by those who had volunteered to serve, but kept regular sketchbooks which they later used as reference for paintings. William Lionel Wyllie was probably the most prolific, versatile and best of the First World War marine artists, for many of his quickly drawn watercolour sketches have qualities which some artists

THE TSS *RUAHINE*
Charles Dixon (1872–1934)
P & O, London

Another strong and impressive ship-portrait painting, again showing the variations in style and technique adopted by Dixon when executing a painting of a named ship for a specific client. In this example the sense of movement is not only maintained by the sailing craft in the foreground, but is further enhanced by the downward direction of the liner's exhaust.

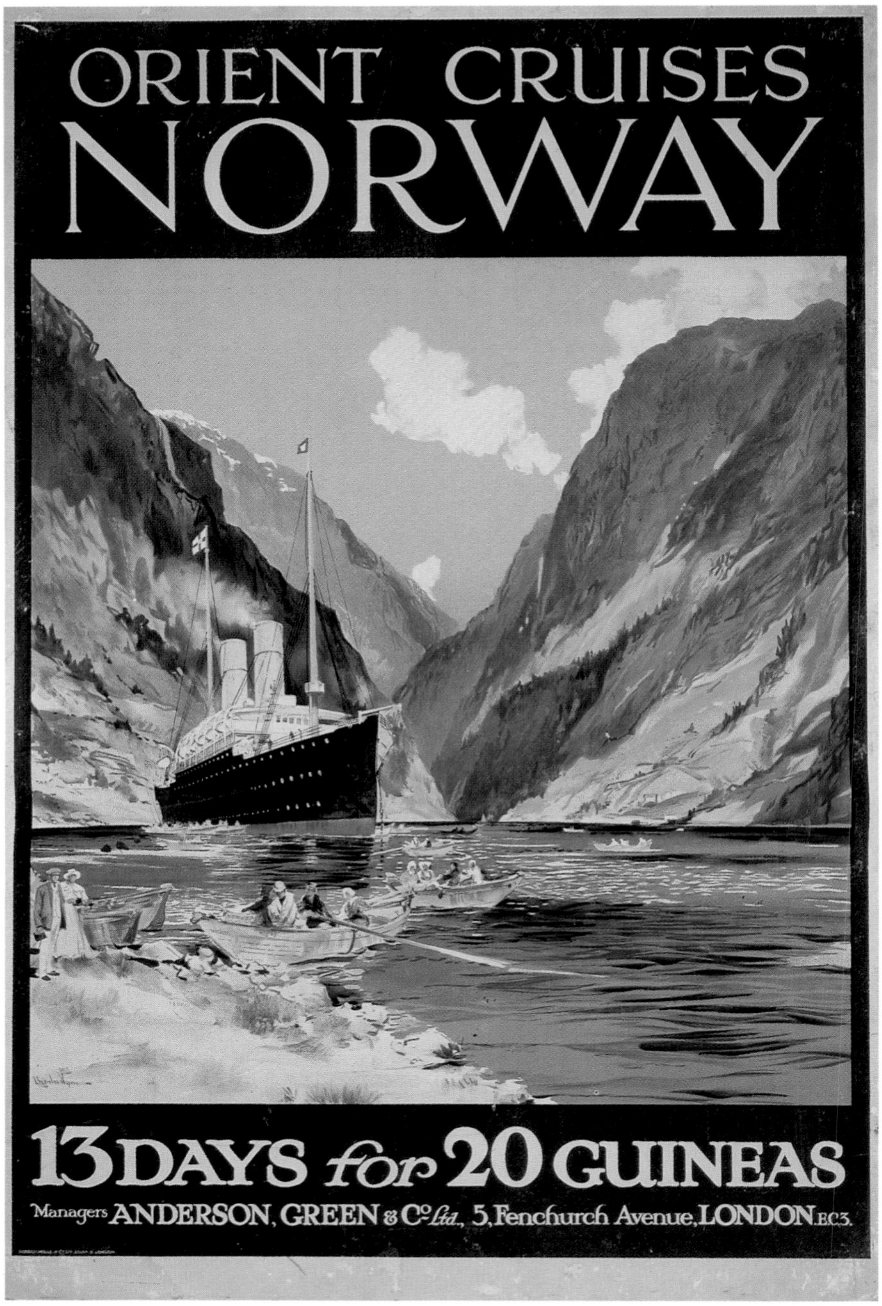

△ *ORIENT* CRUISES NORWAY
Charles Dixon (1872–1934)
P & O, London
This is one of Dixon's watercolour studies designed specifically for use on a poster and reproduced originally by lithography. The treatment is bold and colourful, and Dixon has successfully overcome the compositional problems of the "portrait format" by the juxtaposition of the ship and the mountains.

▷ THE FUTURE "STAR" OF THE WHITE STAR LINE, THE RMS *OLYMPIC* LEAVING SOUTHAMPTON IN 1910
Charles Dixon (1872–1934)
N.R.Omell Galleries, London

The future "Pride" of the White Star Line
Charles Dixon. L.S.C. 1910.

RIGGING A NEW TOPGALLANT YARD
Arthur John Trevor Briscoe (1873–1943)
Royal Exchange Art Gallery, London
Even though the subject may be considered a very technical and therefore specialized aspect from the days of the last of the merchant sailing ships, this watercolour study retains its quality as a painting in its own right. Such detailed observation is rarely seen by modern marine artists, but it was something at which Briscoe excelled, and he always managed to produce a pleasing composition with its help.

have been unable to demonstrate in more highly finished paintings.

During the Second World War, the War Artists' Advisory Committee and the Admiralty both employed marine artists to concentrate on the recording of naval subjects. However, as with some of the artists from the First, there are many which are not so much a historical record of what happened, but rather a visual impression of the effect on the mind of the artist; they therefore lean very much towards the abstract concept of painting. Nevertheless, there were many artists who left excellent historical records which leave any emotional feelings to be formulated in the mind of the viewer. Norman Wilkinson, for example, produced a set of 56 oil paintings of varying quality depicting the war at sea from 1939 to 1945, which he presented to the British nation; the majority are housed in the National Maritime Museum, Greenwich.

POSTERS AND THE LINER AGE

To move around from one part of the country to another, or indeed to move to another country altogether, was more often than not the result of desire to improve one's standing and prospects in life. As the 19th century progressed, an increasing number of people travelled to establish and develop trading links and businesses, but travel for pleasure is a comparatively recent concept. It grew steadily before 1914 and reached a peak in the 1920s and 1930s, when many wealthy individuals took advantage of the competitive, but expensive, opulence provided by the transatlantic liners and the early cruise ships. It was a period of leisurely inactivity, if one had the resources to indulge in it. Indirectly, it also generated further outlets for the work of marine artists through the need for large, colourful posters. This was because it was

THE FOREMAST
Arthur John Trevor Briscoe (1873–1943)
Royal Exchange Art Gallery, London
A beautiful and traditionally rendered watercolour painting vividly conveying the atmosphere of working aloft on a square-rigged sailing ship in the balmy airs of the tropics.

easier to manipulate a drawn image than a photographic one; it was possible for an artist to compose a painting around the very specific requirements of the commissioning company, whereas it might take months to achieve the same effect through photography. This was particularly important as the shipping companies were competing for a relatively small clientele.

Artists employed in such work were given an opportunity to indulge briefly in a more graphic, or design-orientated, approach and also at times to adjust their techniques so that the printing process would more accurately reproduce their work. This type of work was not just restricted to shipping and railway companies, but extended to organizations such as the Empire Marketing

THE SUEZ CANAL
Charles Pears (1873–1958)
Public Record Office, London
One of a series of posters designed and produced by the Empire Marketing Board to encourage the British public to purchase goods from the Empire. When this example is compared with the paintings reproduced earlier by the same artist, it quickly becomes clear that Pears' technique was well suited to reproduction in poster form; the simplicity of shapes, with large expanses of predominantly flat colour, contribute to ensuring a sharp, bold and inspiring image.

Board, established in 1926 to promote the products being produced by the British Empire and encourage the British public to buy them. Many of the posters designed and printed for this board, and often unpublished, are held by the Public Record Office in London, and include some remarkably bright, cheerful and well-designed images by marine artists such as Charles Pears, Charles Dixon (1872–1934), and the little-known, but equally excellent Kenneth Shoesmith (1896–1939).

Claus Bergen

Many people consider marine painting to be nothing more than studies of ships, but nothing could be further from the truth, and if it were more widely understood the genre would receive greater recognition. However, one aspect of the liner paintings I have discussed was that they did encourage artists to compose paintings which had more feeling and life to them than was possible in ship portraits. A good example is Claus Bergen's study on board the German liner *Columbus*. It was painted by Bergen (1884–1965) in 1924 and shows a deck scene on a bright, sunny day, looking along the port side towards the bows, the part of the ship which is visible filling the right-hand side of the painting. To the left is the wash from the liner and open sea, the whole being brought together by the expanse of sky above. Of particular note is the way Bergen has captured the spray created by the wind against the natural flow of the liner's wash, which, with the small exhaust of steam escaping from a pipe abaft the forward funnel, is just sufficient to indicate a fresh breeze blowing and the direction it is coming from. The promenade deck is alive with passenger activity – people playing games, reading, chatting and generally

NAZI WREATH IN THE NORTH SEA IN MEMORY OF THE BATTLE OF JUTLAND
Claus Bergen (1885–1964)
National Maritime Museum, London
This oil painting by a comparatively little-known German marine artist is a beautifully atmospheric study of the relentless sea and sky. It is made all the more powerful and moving not only by the wreath, with its splash of red, but by the amazing sense of depth and distance which the artist has so effectively captured. The whole is enhanced by the luminous glow in the sky and its subtle reflection on the horizon.

enjoying the bracing air. The whole painting is keenly observed and beautifully composed, the unobtrusive and clever focal point to the whole painting being the lonely officer-of-the-watch on lookout on the port bridge wing.

MARIN-MARIE

The great French painter Marin-Marie, born in 1901, was another marine artist who recorded contemporary deck scenes as well as anything else associated with the sea, including ships being overhauled and refitted and even, on occasions, studies of off-watch crew members. However, it is the technique he developed for rendering the sea in watercolour which must make Marin-Marie one of the outstanding marine artists of the century. Remarkably, he was self-taught and equally competent in other media. In 1933 and 1936 he sailed the Atlantic single-handed; he wrote a book about his first journey, *Wind Aloft*, which was published in London in 1947. Contained within it, with no particular bearing on the story, are reproductions of two of his watercolours, one showing a four-masted barque under full sail from the port quarter, with a tramp steamer off towards the horizon on the barque's starboard quarter, the second showing a barque hove-to in the middle distance, offset to the right and with a pilot boat in the left foreground. Both paintings show what would appear to be vessels belonging to A. D. Bordes' fleet. The seas in both paintings are finely executed, and all the more impressive because they are in watercolour, one of the most difficult of media with which to paint the sea. They are the watercolour version of Holst's oil-painted seas. These are not exceptions when examining Marin-Marie's work, for the Musée de la Marine in Paris has many other examples, such as the series he com-

A BLUE STAR CARGO-LINER ON THE OPEN SEA
Norman Wilkinson (1878–1971)
Christie's, London
This is one of Wilkinson's much later paintings of a typical 1950s cargo ship. As can be seen, it shows the development of his open and loose technique, so that this painting is best viewed at a distance. In some respects it is almost bland in its composition and content, but nevertheless it demonstrates one approach in achieving a broad expanse of open space with a modern cargo ship as a principal subject, which is often difficult to achieve convincingly.

pleted of the exploration ship *Pourquoi-Pas?* in the Arctic, which demonstrate his outstanding abilities as a marine artist.

Professional Societies

A particularly important development in marine painting in Britain, which took place in 1939, was the formation of the Society of Marine Artists. The society came about as a result of discussions between a number of artists, including Arthur Briscoe, Charles Pears and Norman Wilkinson. They initiated a number of exhibitions devoted solely to marine painting, the first of which was held in Eastbourne, in southern England, in 1935; the third took place in London in 1937, under the patronage of King George VI, and was opened by Winston Churchill. The group mounted another exhibition in December 1938, but their first exhibition as a clearly defined group did not take place until 1946, with Charles Pears as the first President. They achieved distinction and recognition by the granting of the prefix "Royal" in 1966, and since then have been more commonly known as the RSMA.

A comparable organization, the American Society of Marine Artists, was founded in 1978 under the auspices of the National Maritime Historical Society. It is now recognized as being the leader in the USA, encouraging a greater awareness of America's maritime heritage in its broadest sense, and at the time of writing is thriving, with a well-supported annual exhibition. It has close connections with the RSMA, some artists being members of both

FAREWELL TO *VANGUARD*
Charles E. Turner (1883–1965)
National Maritime Museum, London
Charles Turner was an artist of sometimes variable quality, but this oil sketch of HMS *Vanguard* being towed to the shipbreakers is undoubtedly one of his better and more skilful pieces. It would be interesting to see a wider selection of his rarely reproduced work to determine more clearly his place among 20th-century artists. However, there is no doubt that it was in his ability to produce effective and bold monochrome illustrations for magazines that his greatest strength lay.

societies. However, as a comparatively new organization it is outside the scope of this book; the work of its members, and indeed of those of the RSMA, merits the attention of a separate study to do them justice.

Generally speaking, marine painting in the 20th century developed as a natural extension of that of the latter part of the 19th. In Western Europe and North America it continued to progress in terms of quality until the Second World War, which seems in retrospect to have been a watershed. From then on it has declined, with only a few producing work comparable to that of the great exponents of the first half of the century. With this decline, the demand for modern, but traditional marine painting has also declined. It is therefore fitting that this broadly-based survey on marine painting be drawn to a close in the hope that my wish at the end of my Introduction has been at least partly fulfilled, and that many of my readers will now more fully appreciate a very neglected but important aspect of the history of art.

There are many other marine artists who should be mentioned, but no single volume could ever do justice to marine painting on an international scale. Partly for this reason, the work of some artists is reproduced here, although no mention is made of them in the text, while the reverse is equally true. Omission does not imply criticism of the quality of an artist's work. I hope that this study will help the reader to understand what represents an outstanding example of the marine artist's skill, and thus to formulate his or her own judgement in considering other paintings.

Collecting

MARINE PAINTING, AS A CONSTITUENT OF THE FIELD OF ART AS A whole, is not the most widely studied genre. This makes it difficult to generalize on buying and collecting, especially when one has to take into account geographical variations, which will often influence extreme price variations. Obviously, any outlet, such as a commercial gallery, will adjust its prices according to the type of clientele it is likely to attract; if it is located within a coastal town or harbour, the prices are likely to be higher than inland. Also, the more famous the artist, the higher the price, regardless of the intrinsic quality of the painting. And in the final analysis it is the quality of a painting alone which should tempt a prospective buyer; the price should be a consideration only if it is beyond one's means.

While the national or international standing of an artist affects prices, so, to a lesser extent, does the subject. Invariably paintings of 19th-century clipper ships and other sailing ships have a higher price tag than do paintings of steam warships and merchant vessels. Again, this may be the case regardless of the quality of the image.

On the positive side, it is possible to purchase paintings which are not overpriced, either from galleries or, sometimes, from second-hand bookshops dealing in prints and paintings on a small scale. The serendipity of such visits can be rewarding in itself.

Within the genre of marine painting, all media are and have been practised by artists over the years. Oil paintings tend to dominate at the higher end of the market, at least in price terms, and often regardless of true quality. Watercolours are a close second and can still be purchased for relatively reasonable prices. The more skilled marine artists, associated with the standards of the English School of marine watercolour painting, will however continue to command prices often comparable with those for oils. Acrylics are a comparatively new medium, and many modern marine artists have adopted them with some success; again prices vary, but are more closely related to the standing of the artist.

Engravings remain fairly widely available and low in price, especially through the many galleries specializing in prints, although the number of quality engravings appears to be declining. This is because the technique is little used today, and the masters who excelled in it – primarily from the 17th, 18th and early 19th centuries – left insufficient examples to satisfy contemporary demand. The majority on sale have often been removed from books.

Because many of the inferior-quality engravings represent an early form of mass reproduction, they are not recognized as good examples of the marine artist's skill in the same way as etchings and lithographs. For these it is usually still necessary to visit fine-art galleries, although this is not to suggest that so-called bargains will not be available. Much depends on the individual's taste, as well as on what his or her pocket can afford.

Wash drawings and illustrations produced specifically for reproduction in some of the journals mentioned in earlier chapters are occasionally to be found on the open market; many were sold at public auctions during the 1980s. Works by marine artists who have since become famous are rare, but there remain many by lesser-known artists of comparable quality at reasonable prices.

Pencil studies and sketches by marine artists are rarely to be found. This is a reflection of the attitudes of the institutions housing the great public collections, they are hardly ever considered worthy of placing on public exhibition. Chance finds in secondhand bookshops and back-street print shops are becoming increasingly scarcer, and only the most determined collector would examine closely all that might be on offer in the hope of finding that one single, but worthwhile bargain.

There are a number of galleries which specialize in marine paintings, and many advertise through the journals and magazines associated with maritime history and shipping in general. In the UK the journal of the Society for Nautical Research, *The Mariner's Mirror*, and international magazines such as *Classic Boat, Sea Breezes* and *Ships Monthly* are among some of the more widely known which carry advertisements from specialist galleries. The appreciation of, and therefore the demand for, marine paintings and prints in the USA is higher than in the UK and Europe and therefore the number of advertisements and outlets is greater. US specialist magazines include *American Neptune, Wooden Boat* and *Sea History*. Besides carrying the advertisements, many of these magazines publish articles about specific groups or individual artists, which give a useful introduction to an artist's technique, style and principal subject-matter. The work of contemporary marine artists can be examined through the Royal Society of Marine Artists' and the American Society of Marine Artists' annual exhibitions, in the UK and USA respectively.

PRICE VARIATIONS

Besides the specialist galleries who not only regularly sell marine paintings, but also put on occasional exhibitions of the works of specific artists, there are also national and regional auctions. Presale estimates, intended as a guide for prospective buyers, may have little relationship to the prices being quoted in the specialist galleries for work of a comparable quality by the same artist. This does not mean that buying from one source is necessarily better than the other, and there are many imponderables in the business of buying marine paintings – or indeed *any* paintings – from such outlets. Pricing may well be based on arbitrary decisions and on what little has been published about the genre and those practising it, or even on the size of a painting, however little this may have to do with its quality. At an auction held in London in 1991 a presale price of £4,000–6,000 ($6,800–10,200) was quoted for an oil painting by John Wilson Carmichael, entitled *Becalmed* and executed in 1854. Measuring 20in × 30½in, it was a very mediocre work, lacking in both substance and accuracy. At the same auction, a presale figure of £1,000–1,500 ($1,700–2,550) was quoted for a watercolour painting, 16¼in × 2½in, of the ship *Negotiator* by Nicholas S. Cammilleri, an artist who worked very much in the style of the Roux family. Such comparisons must be to some extent subjective, but the larger work's quality does not appear to justify the price-range given.

At the increasingly popular boat shows and exhibitions held in major cities and in many coastal areas, it is often the small and apparently insignificant private stallholder who can sometimes offer that elusive bargain. There are also students specializing in the more informative and explanatory type of illustration who sometimes offer work of a nautical nature; they are often prepared to sell their work at a far lower price than the professionals, if only to get themselves started.

As a general rule, oil paintings attract far higher prices than watercolours, although it is not easy to see the reason for this, apart from traditional attitudes among both dealers and art historians. The quality and aesthetic beauty of a painting is not of course determined by its medium. The exception to this is again the standing and reputation of the artist.

Variations in prices over the years give a general idea of how the market has developed. A marine watercolour measuring 6in × 19in by that exceptional marine artist William Lionel Wyllie (1851–1931) was sold in London in 1976 for £250 ($425). In 1991 a similarly-sized watercolour by the same artist was priced in the range £1,500–2,500 ($2,550–4,250), while yet another, only fractionally larger, was priced in the range $3,000–5,000 ($5,100–8,500). Besides his exquisite oils and watercolours, Wyllie produced numerous etchings which come onto the market at infrequent intervals. The prices for these vary considerably, according to the gallery selling them and the subject depicted. If the etching is similar in composition and subject to one of his major oil paintings, the price is higher; if a lesser-known class of vessel or subject is involved, the price can be far lower. In the 1980's prices ranged from £100 to £350 ($170 to $595).

As I have mentioned in Chapter Seven, the publication of a major biography of an artist has the effect of increasing the value of his work, because more people are made aware of it. This is the reason why Arthur Briscoe (1873–1943) became popular in 1974 and why his etchings increased in price over subsequent years. As with Wyllie's etchings, prices could be expected to continue to rise simply because a time would eventually come when there would be no more new etchings to sell, even though in both cases some works had quite extensive print runs.

A watercolour by that outstanding 19th-century marine artist, Edward William Cooke (1811–80) was priced at £950 ($1,615) in 1976, which, although quite high at the time, still seems low for a painting by such a notable artist. It is another example of the arbitrary method of pricing marine paintings.

The fact that some artists have few surviving originals on either the open market, or in public or private collections, can also affect the price. John Robert Charles Spurling (1870–1933), the specialist 20th-century painter of 19th-century merchant sailing ships, had many of his originals destroyed during the bombing of London during the Second World War. This has meant that it is extremely rare for any of his works to come up for sale, but when they do the prices are quite extraordinary. In 1990 three original watercolours were sold, one of which had never been reproduced before. They were sold for £3,000 ($5,100), £4,000 ($6,800) and £4,500 ($7,650). Large-sized prints of Spurling's work printed before the Second World War also command very high prices. Prospective purchasers should however beware when buying any form of colour reproduction, because of the fading which occurs when the work is exposed to even a small, but continuous amount of the sun's ultra-violet rays. This fading can take place over a very short space of time, regardless of how accurate and well-printed the image is. The instability of the inks used somewhat negates the concept of buying limited-edition prints for investment. This is equally true of modern prints.

Reproductions, sold under the term "prints", by modern marine artists are possibly the most cost-effective way to build up a small collection. Prices, naturally, vary considerably. Sources for such prints are not only the galleries, but also some of the magazines mentioned above and indeed some of the specialist art journals, including those specially produced for the print market.

The comparatively lower numbers of artists practising marine painting at any time mean that there is less to choose from, at fewer outlets; and, except for contemporary reproductions, the collector must develop an inquisitive and patient nature if he or she is to acquire even a small collection of worthwhile examples.

Index

Bibliography

Space restrictions have prevented a comprehensive bibliography of all sources from being included; those listed represent the more wide-ranging studies.

Archibald, E H H, *Dictionary of Sea Painters*, Suffolk 1980 and 1989
Brewington, M V and Dorothy, *Marine Paintings and Drawings in the Peabody Museum*, Salem 1968
Brook-Hart, Denys, *British 19th Century Marine Painting*, Suffolk 1974
Brook-Hart, Denys, *20th Century British Marine Painting*, Suffolk, 1981
Concise Catalogue of Oil Paintings in the National Maritime Museum, Suffolk 1988
Cordingly, David, *Marine Painting in England 1700–1900*, London 1974
Gaunt, William, *Marine Painting*, New York 1975
Robinson, M S, *Van de Velde Drawings in the National Maritime Museum*, 2 Volumes, Cambridge 1973 and 1974
Robinson, M S, *The Paintings of the Willem van de Veldes*, 2 Volumes, London 1990
Smith, Philip Chadwick Foster, *More Marine Paintings and Drawings in the Peabody Museum*, Salem 1979
Wilmerding, John, *American Marine Painting*, New York 1987

Acknowledgments

While the individuals responsible for the production side of this book are mentioned elsewhere, there are two I would personally like to thank for their support and contribution, having worked closely with them. They are Deirdre O'Day, my picture researcher, who greatly impressed me with her abilities to come up with even more sources of previously unpublished works by artists from my original picture list; and Sally MacEachern, my editor, whose patience and encouragement in coping with my unavoidable delays in submitting sections of the manuscript was greatly appreciated. Working with such people under very tight deadlines is always a bonus!

At the Bournemouth and Poole College of Art and Design, where I lecture, I would like to record a special thanks to Paul Briglin, of the college library, for his assistance and advice in directing me to some of the reference sources which were less directly related to marine painting, but essential in placing the subject in a broader context.

Thanks also to the staff from the School of Computer Aided Art and Design at the college for access to facilities which have helped enormously in the preparation of the text.

Regardless of the pleasure gained from writing a book on a subject which is so close to my heart, the process of writing at home made for an isolated existence, and the encouragement received from Sheila Atkinson, a colleague and friend, is gratefully acknowledged.

My passion for the sea, and in particular the final development of man's most beautiful of creations, the square-rigged sailing ship, which grew from seeing the preserved four-masted barque *Passat* as a nine year old, and which eventually embraced marine painting, has developed in me an appreciation of an art form which has given immense pleasure. It is therefore fitting that the final thanks and acknowledgments should be extended to the artists responsible for giving me that pleasure as a result of their own love of the sea.

Quarto would like to thank the following for providing photographs, and for permission to reproduce copyright material. While every effort has been made to trace and acknowledge all copyright holders, we would like to apologize should any omissions have been made.

Key: a=above; b=below; l=left; c=centre

Abbrevations: CL: (c) Christie's, London; NMM: The National Maritime Museum, London; NRO: Courtesy of N.R. Omell; P&O: Reproduced by courtesy of The Peninsular and Oriental Steam Navigation Company; PMS: Peabody Museum, Salem, Massachusetts/photo Mark Sexton; REG: The Royal Exchange Art Gallery, London.

P 7 NMM **p 8** P&O **p 11** NRO **p 12** REG **p 15** Reproduced by courtesy of the Trustees of the British Museum **p 16** C M Dixon, Canterbury **p 17** b Reproduced by courtesy of the Trustees of the British Museum **p 19** C M Dixon, Canterbury **p 21** The Bodleian Library, Oxford **p 23** Reproduced by permission of the Birmingham Museum and Art Gallery **p 24** CL **p 26–27** CL/photo Mike Fear **p 29** NMM **p 31** NMM **p 32** NMM **p 34–35** CL **p 36–37** NMM **p 38–39** NMM **p 40** CL **p 43** NMM **p 44–45** The Pepys Library, The Master & Fellows, Magdalene College, Cambridge **p 46–47** NMM **p 49** NMM **p 50–51** CL **p 52–53** NMM **p 56–57** REG **p 59** NMM **p 61** PMS **p 62–63** NMM **p 64–65** PMS **p 67** Norfolk Museums Service (Norwich Castle Museum) **p 68–69** PMS **p 72–73** REG **p 74–75** CL **p 77** Guildhall Art Gallery, London/The Bridgeman Art Library **p 78–79** Birmingham Museums and Art Gallery/The Bridgeman Art Library **p 80** Hull Museums and Art Gallery **p 81** NRO **p 82** PMS **p 84–85** PMS **p 86–87** PMS **p 89** REG **p 91** REG **p 92–93** Richard Green Gallery **p 94–95** Tate Gallery, London **p 96** NRO **p 98** Reproduced with permission of the Tyne & Wear Museum (Laing Art Gallery) **p 99** NMM **p 100–101** REG **p 102–103** REG **p 104** Nottingham Castle Museum and Art Gallery **p 105** REG **p 106** Guildhall Gallery, London/The Bridgeman Art Library **p 108** Harris Museum and Art Gallery **p 109** NRO **p 110–111** Tate Gallery, London **p 112–113** REG **p 114** CL **p 115** NMM **p 117** CL **p 119** a CL b Penobscot Marine Museum, Searsport, Maine **p 120** Penobscot Marine Museum, Searsport, Maine **p 121** PMS **p 123** CL **p 124** (c) Addison Gallery of American Art, Phillips Academy, Andover, Massachusetts. All Rights Reserved **p 125** Courtesy of Frank Opple **p 127** NRO **p 129** NRO **p 130** NRO **p 132** NRO **p 134** NRO **p 136** NRO **p 139** CL **p 141** CL **p 143** NMR **p 144** a Deutsches Schiffahrtsmuseum b REG **p 145** REG **p 146–147** P&O **p 148** a P&O b REG **p 149** PMS **p 151** a NMM b REG **p 152–153** NRO **p 154** NRO **p 156** CL **p 157** P&O **p 159** REG **p 160** REG **p 161** NMM **p 162** NRO **p 165** P&O **p 166–67** NMM **p 169** NMM **p 170** NMM **p 171** P&O **p 172** NMM **p 173** PMS **p 174** a REG **p 177** P&O **p 179** P&O **p 180** P&O **p 181** NRO **p 182** REG **p 183** REG **p 184** (c) Public Record Office, London **p 185** NMM **p 186** CL **p 187** NMM.